GARDENS
Maine Style
ACT II

GARDENS
Maine Style
ACT II

Rebecca Sawyer-Fay

Photographs by Lynn Karlin

Rebecca Sawyer-Fay
Lynn Karlin

Down East

To Maine's resilient gardeners
past and present

Library of Congress Cataloging-in-Publication Data

Sawyer-Fay, Rebecca.
  Gardens Maine style : Act II / Rebecca Sawyer-Fay ;
photographs by Lynn Karlin.
    p. cm.
  ISBN 978-0-89272-747-6 (trade hardcover : alk. paper)
  1. Gardens--Maine. I. Title.
  SB451.34.M2S293 2008
  635.09741--dc22

                                    2007041854

Design by Faith Hague Book Design
Printed in China

2   4   5   3   1

Book orders: 1-800-685-7962
www.downeast.com
Distributed to the trade by National Book Network

Contents

Foreword

The Magic of Maine Gardens

"It's just magic!" On our quest for great gardens throughout Maine, we couldn't help but notice how often we heard this exclamation—even from those who know that imagination, careful planning, hard work, and outstanding soil are key to any successful garden. Experienced gardeners know that "abracadabra" has nothing to do with it.

Or does it? Over time, we began to see parallels between gardening and showmanship. For instance, the anticipation and excitement that precede spring have much in common with the hush that falls over an audience just before the curtain rises. Selecting the right plants and creating a suitable backdrop are a lot like finding outstanding players and furnishing them with a set and props. Behind the scenes, a creative gardener, like a stage director, puts it all together in the most effective way possible.

We realized, too, that our favorite gardens transcend the merely pretty, combining visceral pleasure with a deeper relevance. Some of the landscapes featured on the following pages emphasize what we love most about Maine: the rugged coastline and glassy lakes, the massive boulders and indigenous species, the morning fog and dappled evening light, the sleepy valleys where nothing much has changed in generations. Other featured landscapes, graced with historic plants, keep the past alive. When packed with spring-blooming bulbs, they offer hope in hard times. Always, they remind us of what matters most. Now, that's magic!

—*Rebecca & Lynn*

"Helios 1," an illuminated glass sculpture from an exhibit by Eric Hopkins, casts a golden glow at Coastal Maine Botanical Gardens, in Boothbay.

I

Opening Act

The garden awakens

Come April, Maine's ever-hopeful gardeners pull on their boots, grab their leaf rakes, and barely conceal their joy as they head outdoors. Even though the forecast may yet include snow, and the prospect of plants in full bloom seems about as likely as Harry Houdini breaking free of his handcuffs, Maine gardeners forge ahead. Silently, and almost always alone, they begin the annual ritual of taking stock of their losses: the supposedly hardy roses, now utterly gone; the dead-as-a-doornail dogwood, planted so lovingly just a year ago; and of course the lavender, showing no signs of life whatsoever.

Curtain up! As daylight lengthens and the soil warms, snow is no impediment to early-flowering tulips eager to put on a show.

But wait. What's that green shoot poking through the fallen leaves at the base of the mailbox? Bonded with a layer of sand (the municipal aftermath of countless snowstorms), the leaves form a heavy, muddy mat. And then a moment of what can only be called magic: spring's bounty revealed as gloved hands gently pull back the winter carpet. Dozens of newly emergent jonquils, crocuses, and diminutive iris, along with nascent daylilies and bleeding heart, declare that all is not, in fact, lost.

Maine's gardeners do mourn their losses, but they don't dwell on them. There's simply too much to do. And besides, every empty spot in border or bed provides an opportunity to try something new. The persistent ones take heart from another observation: With each passing season, they lose fewer plants. These experienced gardeners have learned from their mistakes. They know that, although much can be blamed on the weather (as well as on voracious deer and rodents), not everything is the result of forces beyond a gardener's control. By following a few rules, they tilt the odds in their own favor. For example, they put the right plant in the right spot—a concept that sounds easy in theory but can be difficult in practice.

Design considerations as well as desire—call it plant lust—not infrequently clash with a gardener's better judgment. A brick path cries out to be edged in English lavender (*Lavandula angustifolia*), a perennial

Opposite: *Hosta* 'Krossa Regal' gives little indication in early spring that by summer its spread will reach a jaw-dropping five feet and its mauve-hued blossoms will grace stalks, or scapes, four feet tall. Named for physician and botanist Nicolaus Thomas Host (1761–1834), the shade-loving perennial takes Maine's winters in stride.

Above: Come spring, not all surprises are welcome. A "tombstone" erected at the end of a brutal winter commemorates the dead in the Northport garden of Jean and Robert Rich.

Left: White grape hyacinth (*Muscari botryoides* 'album') and dainty jonquils (*Narcissus triandrus* 'Lemon Drops') perform a lively, and harmonious, spring duet.

Right: It takes more than blackflies to deter spring shoppers in search of shade-tolerant plants in Swanville, at Fernwood Nursery and Gardens, famous for perennials perfectly suited to Maine's challenging climate.

Below: A Christmas fern (*Polystichum acrostichoides*) unfurls its fiddlehead in early May.

rated hardy to USDA Zone 5, making it viable (all the books say) in Maine's more temperate regions. But the low-lying brick path doesn't drain well, and it's exposed to winter winds. Predictably, the lavender dies. And so it goes.

Hardiness is a relative term, Maine's gardeners quickly learn. Those who purchase plants based solely on USDA zone information court disappointment. A glance at the USDA zone map shows why: Stress resulting from acid rain and other forms of pollution isn't part of the picture; nor is the hardship caused by inadequate snow cover in winter. Without an insulating blanket of snow, perennials are far more vulnerable to temperature fluctuations, ice, disease, and winds that suck the moisture from plant tissues. Unprotected

plants die when temperatures drop dramatically, causing ice crystals to form inside the plant's cells, which then rupture. To mitigate the effects of a no-snow or low-snow winter, savvy gardeners top their plants with a thick layer of leaves or evergreen boughs in late autumn.

These gardeners also know that *when* they plant can be as important as *what* they plant. Planting in July is seldom advised, because heat leads to stress, no matter how often a gardener waters. Spring planting is far better, giving perennials the best opportunity to settle in and put down healthy roots. Late-summer planting is another option—an especially seductive one, because prices at nurseries often drop in September. An early freeze can nullify any savings, however.

Left: Open, sesame: Nursery-propagated Japanese Jack-in-the-pulpit (*Arisaema sikokianum)* came to America in the 1990s and now performs alongside its tuberous native cousin (*A. triphyllum*) in Maine's woodland gardens. In early April, "Jack" (the snow-white spadix) emerges from his burgundy-tinged pulpit (the spathe), to great applause.

Below: Fringed bleeding heart (*Dicentra eximia*), singled out for special merit by the Maine nursery industry, withstands temperatures as cold as −30 degrees F.

Bottom: Its work complete, the seed coat of a butternut squash prepares to exit the scene. Just days ago, the coat concealed a primary root (the radicle), a shoot (the plumule), and the future plant's first leaves (the cotyledons).

Nothing shouts "Spring is here!" quite like forsythia and narcissi. For the street side of her weathered fence, Robin Horty chose 'Avalon' large-cup daffodils, with sturdy stems and long-lasting flowers that hold up nicely in the vase as well as in the garden.

For an "opening act" that extends from the jonquils of April to the rudbeckias of August, gardeners searching for the hardiest plants don't just prowl local nurseries that raise their own stock, and they don't just peer over fences. They canvass the woods for ideas and visit Maine's botanical gardens and arboretums. Here they find ample suggestions for species that thrive without help from anyone. Purchased from reputable nurseries, native or naturalized ferns, primroses, and columbines are good choices. But even native plants aren't foolproof. If the mercury falls precipitously, established plants growing in the wild will likely survive, but native plants propagated in a nursery and newly transplanted into gardens may not. And propagated plants are not inexpensive, owing to the time-consuming work involved. The window for taking cuttings is sometimes just a couple of weeks. Yet with each passing year, prices fall and selection expands—great news for gardeners, as well as for Maine's native plants. They are thus less likely to be pilfered from the wild, a practice that has decimated populations of orchids, trilliums, and mosses.

Although some gardeners admit to a certain defensive pessimism, refusing to purchase any plant that isn't rated at least one zone colder than their own, other gardeners are constantly tempting fate. There are always microclimates, they reason, sheltered spots away from prevailing northeast winds. True, the lavender didn't work along the front path, these undaunted gardeners muse philosophically. But what about that south-facing slope in the lee of the old stone wall? This is Maine, after all. Miracles happen.

Casting Call

Maine's botanical gardens and arboretums offer ideal venues for observing plants in action before you buy. On-site horticulturists and garden staff can often answer questions about unfamiliar species and provide insight regarding what works—and what doesn't—in the Pine Tree State. (All area codes are 207.)

Asticou Azalea Garden, Routes 198 & 3 (Peabody Drive), Northeast Harbor; 276-5130 (www.acadiamagic.com)

Coastal Maine Botanical Gardens, Barters Island Road, Boothbay; 633-4333 (www.cmbg@mainegardens.org)

Lyle E. Littlefield Trial Gardens, University of Maine, Orono; 581–2918 (www.umaine.edu/hc/ornamental.htm)

McLaughlin Garden and Horticultural Center, 97 Main Street, South Paris; 743-8820 (www.mclaughlingarden.org)

Merryspring Nature Center, Conway Road, Camden; 236-2239 (www.merryspring.org)

Pine Tree State Arboretum, 153 Hospital Street (Route 9), Augusta; 621–0031 (www.pinetreestatearboretum.org)

Thuya Garden, Route 3, Northeast Harbor; 276-5130 (www.acadiamagic.com)

Wild Gardens of Acadia, off Route 3, Acadia National Park; 288-3338 (www.acadiamagic.com)

Left: The blossoms of Oriental poppies come "packed so closely that the fine silk of the petals is crushed into a million shapeless wrinkles," John Ruskin wrote in 1888. "When the flower opens, it seems a deliverance from torture."

Top: In midspring, *Iris* 'Honky Tonk Blues', a white-washed medium blue, gets ready to show the world why it won the top prize for tall bearded iris in 1995.

Above: A giant onion (*Allium giganteum*) sheds its filmy tunic in early summer. When fully open in another day or so, deep pink-to-purple floral globes will top stalks three to four feet tall.

Initially delicate in appearance, drought-tolerant rudbeckia will dominate the summer scene in August.

II

Star Performers

Plants that merit top billing

In every garden, as on every stage, one performer often steals the show. Whether through color, habit, scent, or rarity, this show-off will upstage the other players and hold the attention of the audience. Some of these grandstanders do try to get along with the rest of the cast by not monopolizing too much of the gardener's time (think of care-free lilacs, for example). Others, though, are genuine prima donnas (certain roses come to mind), demanding almost constant TLC. Not infrequently, gardeners give in to the "wow" factor and employ their favorite "stars" as focal points.

Double white lilac 'Madame Lemoine'

Other times, a plant's appeal is known only to the person who grows it. An unusual backstory (lady's mantle certainly boasts one), personal associations (the peony we remember having flourished in our grandmother's garden), or simple lust (the fifty-dollar daylily that's just entered circulation) all determine which plants we just cannot live without.

Lilacs link present to past, tying today's landcapes to Maine's earliest pleasure gardens. One whiff is all it takes to transport us back to a time when hard-to-come-by ornamental plants exuded luxury. Native to the Balkans, *Syringa vulgaris* crossed the Atlantic with European emigrants, who went to considerable trouble to bundle the bare-root plants in moistened burlap and pack them in trunks filled with straw or insulating sawdust. Throughout Maine, descendants of these early lilacs remain intact, even though the farmhouses they once graced may have vanished long ago.

Today's gardeners often site lilacs as their pre-decessors did, near doorways and windows, where in late May the fragrance of dense, abundant panicles can filter through every room in the house. But unlike nineteenth-century gardeners, to whom *lilac* meant purple, contemporary lovers of these long-lived shrubs can choose from countless colors and forms, from singles in shell pink and deep garnet to doubles in sky blue and creamy white. Some cultivars ('Sensation' among them) even flaunt petals edged in a contrasting color.

Whereas Maine's renowned antique lilacs often stand twenty feet tall, newer shrubs are considerably shorter and can be counted on to reach five feet in an equal number of years. They need full sun, excellent drainage, and grooming to remove dead wood after major winter storms.

Peonies know how to make an entrance. In June, when the plump buds of herbaceous peonies erupt into

fragrant powder puffs, 'Sarah Bernhardt' and her sisters stand alone. Along with tree peonies (with woody year-round stems) and intersectional peonies (the result of crossing tree peonies with herbaceous varieties), herbaceous peonies grab the spotlight in the late-spring garden. (Bonus: Because they die back completely in winter, herbaceous cultivars can be sited along driveways without fear of snowplow damage.) Blossoms can range from dainty singles to extravagant pompoms in creams, pinks, reds, golds, and bicolors. Best planted in autumn, peonies get off to a slow start (three years on average for herbaceous cultivars and five years for tree form). But patient gardeners—and their grandchildren and perhaps even their great-grandchildren—are often rewarded with decades of unrivaled loveliness.

For maximum fragrance and color, peonies should be given full sun, rich soil, and good drainage. A protected site in the lee of a south-facing wall will help plants withstand bud blast, triggered by Maine's cold, wet springs. When "blasted," the tiny buds blacken, shrivel, and die—a grim sight, although one with consequences less than lethal. The current year's show will not go on, but the plants can, and usually do, rebound in time for next year's performance. To extend the display from two to four or even five weeks, gardeners passionate about peonies plant early, middle, and late varieties.

Candelabra primroses (*Primula* X *bulleesiana*) never fail to enchant. So why aren't they more widely grown? Simple confusion may be one reason. A complex genus encompassing more than four hundred species, primulas are often associated with the tender bedding types in flashy colors laid out in quantity at superstores every April. The hardy perennial types are something else entirely. They're much more subtle, with diminutive, fragrant blossoms of pink, mauve, and magenta borne in early summer.

Another reason: So-called candelabra primroses (named for their whorls of blossoms on sturdy two-foot stems that resemble candelabra) must be made happy if they are to flourish, set seed, and create ever-larger colonies of vigorous plants. Damp or (better yet) boggy soil that's rich, peaty, and slightly acidic is a must. Dappled shade will help roots stay cool and mimic the moist mountain meadows where the plants originated. Although direct seeding is possible, it's safer to start seeds indoors in late winter, or purchase Maine-raised plants from a Maine nursery and let them self-seed once established. Bog plants such as marshmallow and skunk cabbage provide a stunning backdrop.

Siberian irises don't come from Siberia. They're native to central Europe, but the name is an apt indicator of this rhizomatous perennial's suitability to Maine's gardens. Frigid temperatures are no problem, and neither is soil that's often acidic (a result of the state's coniferous forests). The plants' graceful, long-season foliage is handy for camouflaging spent daffodils. And Siberian irises make no complaints about partial shade. They do need water on a regular basis, however, especially during the first few years.

Above: Candelabra primroses (*Primula* x *bulleesiana*)

Thanks to Dr. Currier McEwen, a towering figure in the world of iris hybridization, Siberian irises are now a Maine icon, much like birch trees and lady's slipper orchids. At his home in Harpswell, Dr. McEwen bred the first yellow Siberian as well as the first tetraploid (with fuller blossoms, owing to its genetic makeup: a fourfold increase in the number of chromosomes). Enraptured with the plants and inspired by Dr. McEwen's many achievements, a new generation of hybridizers is keeping Maine in the forefront of innovation—and gardeners supplied with the latest cultivars.

Above: 'Miss Portland', a Dunlop & Cole Siberian iris hybrid

Left: Siberian iris hybridizers Jeff Dunlop (left) and Dean Cole look for standouts among Dean's older seedling rows in Gorham. Every June, about two thousand new plants transform their two gardens into oceans of blues, purples, and creams. The newest and best selections are sold through Fieldstone Gardens, in Vassalboro.

Lady's mantle works its magic at daybreak, when dewdrops collect in the creases of the palmate foliage. A quick look around at neighboring plants shows just how unusual a trait this is. It also explains how the perennial earned its Latin name: *Alchemilla*, literally "little magical one" (the common name arose from the leaves' resemblance to a cloak). To medieval alchemists, the dewdrops (collectively called "celestial water") looked like tiny pearls and were favored ingredients in experiments to turn base metals into silver and gold. The plant's ability to self-fertilize and reproduce without the help of insects also drew the attention of these early experimenters.

Today's gardeners don't care that early hopes for lady's mantle were dashed. They use the unfussy, freely spreading plants in rock gardens and as a drought-

Lady's mantle (*Alchemilla erythropoda*)

tolerant ground cover. In lieu of expensive, slow-to-grow, and high-maintenance boxwood, lady's mantle makes a handsome frame for mixed borders (just be sure to snip off the pretty sulfur-yellow flowers before the seed has a chance to spread). Easy to propagate by root division, lady's mantle is a common sight at community plant sales throughout the state. This is a good opportunity for gardeners to purchase quantities inexpensively to cover large areas and hold the soil on hillsides and embankments.

Lady's slipper orchids are simply too gorgeous for their own good. Over the years, vandals have poached so many of the sensitive plants from Maine's public lands that *Cypripedium reginae* (known commonly as showy lady's slipper) is now on the state's list of threatened plants. Thieves yank the six-inch-tall natives from the wild in the mistaken belief that they can be easily transplanted. This seldom works, owing in part to the plants' symbiotic relationship with microorganisms in the soil. Pilferage, along with habitat destruction, has taken a heavy toll.

Savvy gardeners know they needn't harm wild colonies to enjoy "showys" and other North American native orchids. Maine's specialty nurseries now offer a wide range of nursery-propagated lady's slippers. Although each species has its own cultural requirements, for the most part these irresistible beauties fare best under hardwood trees, where they can soak up the energy of early-spring sunshine before the trees leaf out, then benefit from cooling shade later in the season. Consistent moisture is important, because the shallow root systems, which extend as far as three feet in each direction, must not be allowed to dry out. Lady's slippers look especially attractive interplanted with ferns, hostas, and marsh marigolds at the edge of a stream, which helps roots stay cool and hydrated.

Because propagating orchids from seed can take as long as seven years and requires sterile laboratory conditions to avoid bacterial contamination, lady's slippers aren't inexpensive. But they come with the prospect that Maine's ever-shrinking wild orchid colonies may persist for future generations to enjoy.

Top: Alaskan lady's slipper (*Cypripedium guttatum*)

Bottom: 'Showy' lady's slipper (*Cypripedium reginae* 'Showy')

Roses rightly qualify as the prima donnas of the garden. They whine about most everything: cold temperatures, bitter winds, pests, dampness, dryness—you name it, it's a cause for complaint. But although the roses may grouse, their devotees do not. Those who have fallen under the spell of the genus *Rosa* will try, try, and try again. Eventually, they learn the three cardinal rules of growing roses: (1) buy own-root (as opposed to grafted) roses; (2) plant in full sun in rich soil amended with plenty of compost; and (3) water deeply and often. Gardeners who play it safe choose tough rugosas and vigorous hybrids (including those in the Canadian Explorer series and those bred by Dr. Griffith Buck). But many gardeners don't hold

Top left: David Austin English rose 'Golden Celebration'

Right: 'William Baffin' roses smother the Belfast cottage of Dr. George Holmes. This ultra-tough climber is one of a series of roses named for Canadian explorers and developed in Germany by Wilhelm Kordes.

Left: *Rosa* 'William Baffin'

back, believing that the rewards of temptresses such as 'Mme. Hardy' (a pristine white damask) and 'Hermosa' (a bright mid-pink China) are worth any effort and expense.

The truly adventurous try their hand at David Austin's English roses, with their seductive, fully cupped, old-rose form and often heady scent. Temperate coastal sites protected from winter winds offer the best chance of success, especially with the vigorous 'Graham Thomas' (a warm yellow), the perpetually blooming 'Mary Rose' (deep pink), and the apricot-pink 'Cressida' (especially hardy, owing to its rugosa parentage).

The pampering doesn't stop when the curtain drops. In late autumn, many hybrid roses make one final demand: a blanket of soil or compost to cover the crown, and a layer of straw and evergreen boughs to hold the blanket in place. Some rosarians, including Bob Bangs, of Windswept Gardens in Bangor, prefer the two-cone method: After cutting back canes to about twelve inches, they slice off the top of a Styrofoam cone and use the base to cover the rose. They pour soil through the top opening, then place a second cone (with top intact) over the first. A brick balanced on top secures the mini shelter against high winds. On warmer than usual winter days, when rising temperatures threaten plant dormancy, the outer cone can be removed to allow the plant to chill down, then be replaced when the mercury falls once more.

Top: Daylily 'Amelia Sophia', hybridized by Susan Shaw

Left and opposite: Susan Shaw, one of many daylily hybridizers in Maine, collects pollen from cultivars in her Camden garden and stores the tiny grains in pill trays. She transfers the pollen to the stigmas of selected partners, then waits for pods to develop and ripen. The shiny black seeds inside will be stored in the refrigerator over winter, then planted the following spring; in three or four years, the first true blossoms of a new hybrid will appear.

Daylilies (*Hemerocallis* spp.) provide living proof that the free lunch does, in fact, exist. In exchange for minimal care, gardeners receive long-season foliage, tolerance of drought and temperature extremes, and blossoms in just about every color except blue (hybridizers are working on that). Daylilies are adaptable, as well: Happy in relaxed settings on hillsides or along driveways, they also look good in formal schemes. Best of all, they spread cheer late into the season while giving overworked gardeners a much deserved break.

Today's sumptuous varieties have nothing in common with the all-orange "ditch lilies" of old. Over the past half century, amateur as well as professional hybridizers (including members of the Maine Daylily Society) have developed ever more spectacular blossoms in hues both subtle and shocking. Maine hybrids, for example, run the gamut from creamy white and soft yellow to neon-tangerine and shocking pink. Sepals may be ruffled, crinkled, or sprinkled with "diamond dust," a refractive texturing that enhances the play of light on petals.

Unfussy as to soil or food (although the occasional spadeful of horse manure is always welcome), daylilies do like full sun. They multiply quickly via rhizomes, which can be lifted and divided every few years, resulting in ample gifts for friends and community causes—a lot of beauty for little effort.

Right: Dahlia tubers dug in autumn are divided in preparation for winter storage.

Opposite: Phil and Karen Clark's Endless Summer Flower Farm, in Camden, features two hundred dahlia varieties. A thousand cut flowers are sold at the farm each week.

Left: Dahlia (Waterlily form 'Sweet Content')

Dahlias that dazzle come in many guises. Pink Pompons and crimson Collarettes, peachy Waterlilies, and yellow Singles are treasured for their usefulness as cut flowers as well as their ability to wake up the late-season garden. Gardeners with an eye for the gaudy go for giant Cactus dahlias, with spiky bicolored petals radiating from a vivid center. More restrained but equally loved are dainty Mignonettes, with ball-shaped blossoms measuring just two inches across. Initial forays into the world of dahlias can be overwhelming (Which one should I choose?). Soon enough, reticence turns into addiction (I *know* I can find room for just one more!).

Native to Central America, dahlias are raised in Maine as annuals. Many are no more expensive than a six-pack of wax begonias and can similarly be discarded at season's end; they don't have to be lifted and stored over winter. On the other hand, frugal gardeners can enjoy their favorite varieties indefinitely. In autumn, after frost has blackened the foliage, plants should be cut down and tubers dug up carefully (the "eyes" are easily damaged), then rinsed and dried in the sun. Tubers (which can be divided with a sharp knife in either autumn or spring) will survive the winter nicely if stored in boxes filled with straw or sawdust and placed in a frost- and rodent-free cellar or barn. Replanting in spring is best done when the soil is consistently warm.

Top: Hardy hibiscus (*Hibiscus moscheutos* 'Lord Baltimore')

Bottom: Pitcher plant (*Sarracenia* 'Judith Hindle')

Hardy hibiscus (*Hibiscus moscheutos*) add an unexpected touch of the tropics to the Northeast. Used singly as specimens or en masse at the back of borders and along foundations, these two-and-a-half- to four-foot-tall herbaceous beauties look more like exotic shrubs than winter-hardy perennials. Flowers the size of salad plates resemble hollyhocks (the old-fashioned single ones) and are among the largest of any seen in Maine. Although they last little more than a day, others follow in quick succession. Blossoms range from white to mauve to scarlet. From mid-July through September, when June's fireworks have long passed, hardy hibiscus give the garden pizzazz.

Full sun, regular watering, and good air circulation yield flowers with the most intense coloration. They'll also discourage bugs from congregating (Japanese beetles can be a problem). In late autumn, woody stems should be cut back to approximately three inches and the plant mulched with fallen leaves.

Pitcher plants (*Sarracenia* spp.) intrigue with their unusual coloration and highly specialized tubular throats. Hungry insects, including wasps, moths, and flies, that venture too far into the liquid-filled flute seldom make it back out. Wings and legs become entangled in downward-facing hairs, then stick to the plant's coated interior. In seconds, all hope of escape is dashed. Minerals and nitrogen from the bugs' decomposing bodies nourish the carnivorous perennial, making up for the soggy, nutrient-poor soil in which *Sarracenia* thrive.

Maine's native *Sarracenia purpurea* (named for its purple foliage) can be spotted along streams and in bogs. They do not transplant well and thus should be enjoyed right where they are. For gardeners bitten by the *Sarracenia* bug, exotic-looking hybrids can be found at specialty nurseries and through the mail. These tender cultivars make dramatic focal points on sunny terraces, patios, and decks, where curious children (and adults) watch for the doomed.

Sarracenia do well in containers filled with a fifty-fifty mixture of peat moss and perlite, which must be kept constantly moist. To ensure that the roots don't dry out, potted specimens should be placed in shallow pans of rainwater. When cold weather arrives, cultivars rated hardy to Zone 5 can be "planted" (pot and all) in a protected corner of the garden (soil should reach just to the pot's rim). Come spring, the container should be lifted, the plants repotted (to aerate the roots), and the old foliage removed. By late spring, the curtain will rise again on one of the plant world's most captivating dramas.

Dragon's eye pine (*Pinus densiflora* 'Oculus-draconis') refuses to be ignored—it simply will not sit quietly among the other conifers that form the background of many a Maine garden. On each branch tip, alternating bands of yellow and cream give the otherwise green needles a fairytale quality. This Japanese red pine grows slowly, reaching twenty-five feet in about fifteen years. Planted in full sun, it stands up to winter, faring especially well against high winds along the Maine coast. Japan's samurai warriors, who knew a thing or two about tough, reportedly planted red pines near their front doors.

To promote branching, candles (branch tips) should be pruned when still young. Pruning also promotes more variegation, because the "dragon's eye" effect is most pronounced when the needles are immature. In winter, when variegation fades, the tree still offers plenty of interest, with a twisted trunk and richly textured bark that starts out orange-red and ages to gray. Dragon's eye pines like plenty of sun and slightly acidic, well-drained soil.

From a distance, Dragon's eye pine (*Pinus densiflora* 'Oculus-draconis') looks much like any other long-needled pine, but up close its "eyes" stand out clearly.

Red-vein enkianthus (*Enkianthus campanulatus*) may look like a deciduous shrub, but actually it's a quick-change artist. In spring, this eight- to fifteen-foot Japanese native flaunts umbels of dainty light pink to rosy red that dangle temptingly among emerald green leaves. The shrub's autumn costume couldn't be more different, with yellow-, orange-, or garnet-hued foliage (depending on the cultivar) providing the backdrop for golden seedpods arranged in clusters. Planted in pairs—one on either side of an arbor, for example—these highly decorative shrubs look like debutantes in search of a party.

Just as their cousins the rhododendrons do, enkianthus prefer acidic soil with good drainage. A site that's sunny in the morning and partly shaded in the afternoon is ideal. In late winter, deadwood and branches that cross should be removed to keep the shrubs tidy and looking neatly layered. Excellent in woodland gardens, the slow-growing plants team up nicely with rhodies, azaleas, and Solomon's seal. Not least among their many virtues is disease resistance—yet another reason enkianthus have become known as the glamour girls of the spring and autumn garden.

Paper birch trees (*Betula papyrifera*) evoke Maine's history while providing a valuable landscape design element. Well before the first lumberjacks arrived on the scene, the state's indigenous peoples used the bark of paper birch to build canoes and wigwams. Later, the light-colored, straight-grained wood came in handy for everything from toothpicks (Maine's last toothpick factory shut down in 2003) to clothespins, as well as ice-cream sticks and industrial pallets.

Artists and garden designers love the trees, too. Generations of landscape painters and printmakers have found inspiration in the stands of birch that encircle lakes and fringe rivers. In the winter garden, snow white paper birches add texture and brightness to gray days. They're also useful in linking a house with the surrounding woods.

Climate change, pollution, and the dreaded bronze birch borer have made birch-tree cultivation

Red-vein enkianthus (*Enkianthus campanulatus*) in spring (top) and autumn, when dainty deep-pink bells turn into golden pearls

Paper birch
(*Betula papyrifera*)

more challenging than it used to be. Although no environmentally friendly remedy for a borer infestation yet exists, preventative steps can help reduce the risk of one. When purchasing trees, beware of bulges on the bark, a sign that borer larvae have been feeding underneath. Remember, too, that stressed trees are more susceptible to infestation than healthy ones. Because thirst causes stress, trees should be watered regularly during times of drought. Root compaction is something else to monitor. When siting a new house or an outbuilding among birches you hope to keep, watch the movements of people and machines: All it takes is one pass with a tractor or backhoe to compress, and kill, a birch tree's root system.

Poor pruning is yet another potentially fatal mistake. Avoid any work on birches during the spring, when the sap is running; pruning in July or later is safer. Cuts should never be flush with the trunk, as an injured branch collar can provide entry to insects and disease. Unwelcome pruning assistance may come from porcupines and beavers, which like nothing better than birch trees to hone their teeth and build their dams. The base of waterside birches should be wrapped in chicken wire before it's too late.

III

Setting the Scene

How the pros design for drama

A spectacular performance demands a dramatic backdrop—and a great director. In Maine, the backdrop can be ready-made, in the form of a shoreline or a mountain range. More often, though, the stage is set with splendid results by gardeners who live nowhere near picturesque ponds, snug harbors, or sweeping vistas. But no matter where Maine's most memorable gardens are located, they have a lot in common. A strong sense of place is just one characteristic shared by inland and coastal gardens.

Japanese wisteria cloaks an arbor near
Maine's southern coast, transforming a gravel path
from the ordinary to the sublime.

A picturesque harbor serves as focal point for island beds of carefully tended perennials.

Pre-existing features (native hardwoods and conifers, wildflowers and mosses, boulders and rock outcroppings) are factored into the garden's design rather than eradicated from it. Although some clearing of land is often unavoidable when a new garden is created, wise gardeners wait a year or even two before they call in the Bobcats. Learning the lay of the land (Where does the sun rise and set? Where does the snow melt first in spring? Where does water collect?) and what already grows there (possibly such treasures as trillium and lady's slipper) is essential to determining what should—and should not—be eliminated. Not infrequently, these existing features become the starting point around which the garden is designed. An enormous moss-covered boulder, for instance, might prove the centerpiece for a Japanese-inspired landscape, or a stately two-hundred-year-old white pine may shelter a romantic backyard hideaway filled with lilies and hardy roses.

A backdrop of forest and ocean gives Elsie Freeman's coastal garden a strong sense of place. Borders 150 feet long (cared for with help from Gail MacPhee) display an impressionistic mix of poppies, foxgloves, rhododendrons, and more.

Great bones are another hallmark of the gardens we can't forget. Whatever their style—formal or casual, grand or intimate—such gardens have handsome, year-round structure. The same boulders and evergreens that give the garden its sense of place can be counted on to hold the snow in winter and to provide a framework for plants of lesser stature. Man-made structures, including arbors and fences, are part of this all-important skeleton, often doubling as supports on which roses and clematis can climb. Creating year-round structure takes time: A charming bentwood trellis or a brick path can be executed in a single season, but many years must pass before trees and shrubs reach their optimal dimensions. So a patient gardener is something else all great gardens must have.

For a client's island garden, Kathie Iannicelli planted natural-looking swaths of drought-tolerant rose campion, daisies, catmint, lamb's ears, and yarrow, which complement indigenous evergreens and the ocean beyond. Owing to stiff northeast winter winds, perennials are cut to the ground and mulched with seaweed in late autumn. Many plants were chosen for their glaucous foliage, which plays up the silvery light typical of Maine's coastal settings.

Left: Planted in the 1940s and pruned every three weeks in summer, these undulating yews lend formal elegance and year-round structure to a garden on the southern coast of Maine.

Below: In rural Strong, nestled in the state's western mountain region, a centuries-old white pine ties Carolyn and David Jenson's Maine Cottage Garden nursery to the past. A rose-bedecked arbor connects it to the present.

Focal points figure strongly in gardens humble or grand. Professional landscape designers and accomplished home gardeners use them to center the view and tell the eye where to go next. Since ancient times, sculpture, urns, and benches have been used for this purpose. Today, marble goddesses and settees have been joined by specimen trees and shrubs, and vines and climbers trained on arbors or pergolas. Gardeners use these and other treasures to convey their personality and interests, employing everything from weathervanes to locally crafted oversize urns to express themselves. (Caution is advised, however: Too many focal points can be confusing.) "Borrowed" views, which incorporate off-site visual elements while giving a garden a sense of permanence, often eliminate the need for any supplemental decoration. Harborside gardens that overlook lobster boats and buoys need no ornamentation, nor do terraced landscapes backed by mountain peaks.

Opposite: In a former orchard on the midcoast, junipers clipped into spirals draw admiring glances even in the "off" season. To make a pattern for pruning, Gayle Sand Norton suspended a ribbon from the top of each tree, spiraled it downward, then snipped accordingly.

Below: "Woodies" with gnarled branches and craggy bark, like these snow-dusted apple trees, ensure a winter landscape with a beauty all its own.

Paths to Paradise

A garden without a path is like a house without a front door. Sure, you can find your way inside, but the journey isn't nearly as satisfying. Paths show us where to plant (on either side of them) and where to go (to the end, of course). They telegraph a garden's style, be it formal (with bricks neatly laid or stones finely cut) or informal (gravel or pine needles convey a relaxed mood perfectly). In addition to contributing permanent, year-round structure, a well-built path supplies a context for current, and future, growth.

Below: On Mount Desert Island, paired planks allow visitors to explore gently groomed woods without leaving footprints.

Above: Emblematic of the Pine Tree State, conifer needles lend a sense of place to a path banked in hostas. At the path's end, a Maine-made Lunaform urn makes a handsome focal point. Terry and Dianne Hire designed this section of their Northport garden with an eye toward color that's subtle yet rich and infinitely varied.

Top: Which way to go? Flagstones keep feet dry while giving visitors plenty of options for viewing perennials, specimen trees, and shrubs.

Above: Dianthus and pansies spill onto a tidy brick walkway designed by Thomas Lovejoy for a farm in York County. Perennials soak up warmth from the bricks, accelerating their growth.

Left: A path remarkable for its simple yet elegant geometry sounds a formal note in an island landscape designed by the owner.

Opposite: The repeated, sinuous pattern of path and topiary (*Thuja occidentalis,* or American arborvitae) gives Thomas Lovejoy's Cape Neddick garden a sense of rhythm. A landscape architect, Lovejoy set the scene on multiple levels, from low-growing hostas to taller queen-of-the-prairie (*Filipendula rubra*) to climbing hydrangeas.

Above: With its fleet of visiting pleasure boats, Belfast's working waterfront offers an ever-changing backdrop, or "borrowed view," for long-season daylilies, bee balm, phlox, dianthus, and mallow in the garden of Lillian Rose.

Left: A six-foot trellis does double duty, providing privacy in summer and a focal point in winter, when snow clings to "windowpanes." Bland Banwell chose lilacs, including nearly white 'Primrose', for her all-purpose screen in this midcoast garden.

Top: In southern Maine, a banner weathervane mounted on a steeple-like base centers a formal garden designed by Thomas Lovejoy. Spheres (Korean mountain ash) and cones (dwarf Alberta spruce) highlight the thirty-six-by-ninety-foot courtyard's symmetrical layout. Trees no taller than twelve feet and a limited color palette suit the scale of the confined space.

Right: On the midcoast, Queen Anne's lace blankets a meadow where livestock once grazed. Ann and Hugh Aaron mow their ultra-low-maintenance "ungarden" twice each year, in early July and late October.

Above: Raised beds framed in pressure-treated two-by-eights solved a drainage problem for Frank and Janie Vogt in Bethel. Annual volunteers (*Nigella damascena* and *Papaver somniferum* among them) and a home-made cedar arbor festooned with hardy red 'Henry Kelsey' roses give this cottage garden easygoing flair.

The thoughtful use of color is another attribute shared by gardens that linger in our memories. Unfortunately, this subject is often fraught with anxiety, especially for those who fear breaking The Rules. These gardeners can now relax. Long gone are the days when the use of "clashing" or "garish" colors consigned the unwitting to horticultural Siberia. What counts is not "taste" but intention. What effect am I after? What response do I hope to elicit? Shall it be intense primaries or soft pastels? Cool blues or warm reds? Gardeners study how colors appear at different times of the day, when plants are bathed in morning sun or backlit in the late afternoon. Increasingly, gardeners recognize the value of green, a color of immeasurable subtlety and variation. Paradoxically, the tendency to take green for granted shifts the spotlight from the hue itself and places it on foliage texture, form, and movement. An all-green garden can thus be a tranquil yet stimulating oasis in which ornamental grasses capture the slightest breeze and the broad emerald-and-cream leaves of Hosta 'Sundancer' contrast with the palmate foliage of Tiarella 'Pink Pearls'. Brought together by a gardener with an eye for the unconventional, borders composed entirely of foliage prove that green is not one color but many.

Top: In Sullivan, artists Paul and Ann Breeden chose an all-green theme comprising moss-covered boulders, hostas, and ferns to set the scene at Willowbrook Garden and Spring Woods Gallery. Paul transplanted various mosses from elsewhere on the property, being careful to match soil conditions at the new site with those at the old. Depending on the species, a skim-coating of moistened peat or a slurry of barnyard manure can help the moss get a foothold on rocks.

Bottom: Sun-loving ornamental grasses take the place of more traditional shrubbery around the foundation of a house in York. Landscape designer Jacquelyn Nooney mixed blue oat grass (*Helictotrichon sempervirens*) with variegated zebra grass (*Miscanthus sinensis* 'Zebrinus') and taller maiden grass (*M. s.* 'Gracillimus') for a look at once eye-catching and unexpected. Blades sway with the slightest breeze, and colors shift subtly as shadows lengthen at day's end.

Right: Vibrant primary colors pulsate at Stonewall Kitchen, in York. Green foliage breaks up blocks of strong reds, yellows, and blues, turning down the heat. Five-year-old Louisa pays a "complement."

Above: A four-foot-tall Japanese-style fence and rustic gate wrap a Thomaston garden designed by Lee Schneller for Linda Leonard and Philip DiGiovanni. In place of the bamboo used for similar fences throughout Japan, Schneller culled wild spirea from a marshy field and layered it between rows of cedar posts staggered and set two inches apart. More than twenty native plant species, as well as Japanese maples, fill the intimate space.

Gardens we love all have a final element in common—not with one another but with their owners: They evolve. Although costly and time-consuming hardscapes may last "forever," the trappings they showcase are ever-changing, adapting and growing along with the person who planted them. As Maine's late, great plantswoman Marion Hosmer once observed, gardeners planting their first beds and borders focus on colorful annuals. Before long they discover perennials. Then they move on to shrubs, and eventually they sing the praises of trees. Setting the scene can thus entail a lifetime of experimentation. Like impresarios who refine a theatrical production and then refine it some more, true gardeners know that each season brings fresh opportunities in the quest for perfection.

Top: A limited spectrum of greens and golds takes the emphasis off color and places it on foliage, form, and texture. Designer Jacquelyn Nooney used curly parsley to dress up the base of tender needle grass (*Nassella* spp.), backed in turn by tropical elephant's ears (triangular *alocasia* and, to its right, larger *colocasia*).

Bottom: Rescued in the 1970s from a developer's backhoe, 'Cortland' apple trees lend their strong lines to the garden that Marion Hosmer created for her family in southern Maine. Gnarled with time, fruit trees such as these offer some of the best garden "bones."

The Power of Blue

What is it about blue that makes it the most popular color in America? Is it the feeling of serenity it engenders? Could it be the allusion it makes to endless skies and boundless oceans? Gardeners have their own reasons for extolling blue. They know that blue-flowering plants help a small space appear larger. Unlike red, which advances toward the viewer, blue recedes, creating the illusion of depth and distance. Handy, too, is blue's ability to subdue just about any setting: In a garden packed with disparate elements— plants, furnishings, and perhaps the neighbor's roofline—blue evokes order amid chaos. It calms the senses, and the scene, too.

Clockwise from top left: *Campanula persicifolia* (peach-leaved bellflower); *Salvia patens* 'Cambridge Blue'; *Meconopsis grandis* (Himalayan blue poppy), happy in Zone 5; a settee wrapped in roses

IV

Presto!

Quick and easy container gardens

Whether they spend the gardening season at a shorefront cottage or a backwoods camp, some gardeners know that you don't need to turn over a single spadeful of earth to enjoy spring pansies, summer lilies, and autumn asters. Even vegetables and herbs can be grown without tilling the soil. These master illusionists may not have a lot of land (indeed, they may not have any), and they often don't have much free time. But they do have an ace up their collective sleeve: containers of all sizes and descriptions.

The view says "Maine," but the pot says "tropics."
With containers, gardeners can provide a touch of the unexpected,
and experiment with non-hardy plants—even bougainvillea.

Above: Furnished with potted begonias, Mexican heather, mums, and a statuesque dracaena, a patio becomes a verdant extension of the house. In Belfast, Laura and Blaine Richardson installed a Mexican *chiminea* so they can enjoy their intimate garden room on chilly autumn evenings.

Right: An antique trough that once quenched the thirst of hardworking horses now serves as a centerpiece at the Rangeley Public Library. Heidi Ferguson filled the century-old treasure with festive marigolds, snapdragons, and ageratum.

Opposite: A planter assembled from weathered boards and mounted on decorative concrete feet reflects the unpretentious spirit of writer Leslie Land's midcoast garden. Lilies, a fuchsia trained as a standard, Abyssinian gladiolus, trailing *Helichrysum petiolare* 'Limelight', and flowering vines fill the generous eight-foot by twenty-inch box. Inside, a layer of gravel prevents roots from affixing themselves to the wood.

Antique cachepots and imported terra-cotta tubs, ersatz neoclassical planters, and humble whiskey casks sawed in half all serve the purpose. These gardeners have something else, too: imagination to spare, as they pair one-of-a-kind pots with out-of-the-ordinary plants.

Container gardens have virtues that go way beyond simple good looks. In Maine, where in-ground spring planting can get off to a slow start, containers give gardeners a jump on the season: Unlike the soil underfoot, a bag of potting mix doesn't need to thaw.

As soon as temperatures no longer dip below freezing, planters can be packed with just about anything—colorful primroses, exotic elephant's ears (*Colocasia* and *Alocasia*), or the sweetest cherry tomatoes. (Many vegetable and fruit varieties have been bred specifically for container culture.) Vacationers who rent a cottage or camp for just a few weeks can get in on the act, too: Potting up a few herbs and six-packs of nasturtiums takes next to no time, and the mini gardens can be enjoyed immediately.

Gardeners eager to get off their knees appreciate the ease of container care. Recycled crates, beat-up buckets rescued from the dump, even decommissioned rowboats can be used to display plants off the ground, thus sparing backs and sacroiliacs. Other containers have an added attraction: Deer can't reach them. Plants in window boxes affixed to second-story windows, or in pails suspended from tall posts, are seldom nibbled.

Compact and well defined, containers make a virtue of their very limitations. Experimenting with unfamiliar species becomes especially appealing when you know that your mistakes won't cost a fortune.

Tropicals from bougainvillea to brugmansia, and tender perennials from rose-scented geranium (*Pelargonium capitatum*) to cape primrose (*Streptocarpus* spp.), are all viable candidates. If, to your eventual regret, you position flashy red-and-white *Salvia greggii* 'Hot Lips' alongside orange black-eyed Susan vine, you needn't live with your mistake for long; next year's combination can always be more subtle (or not). Gardeners can also choose to tend their pots and planters year-round, greeting each season with a fresh look, from spring's first snowdrops to yuletide's joyful boughs and berries.

Painted sap buckets suspended from cedar posts dress up a deer fence. At Sue Keating's Sweet Pea Gardens, in Surry, Bambi has a tough time reaching red *Calibrachoa*, yellow *Bidens*, and pink lantana.

Above: A simple dish of white impatiens is the only ornamentation required when you have an ancient oak to frame the view. The deck of a 1950s cottage on Mount Desert Island was designed to accommodate the magnificent tree.

Left: A trio of whisky barrels, packed with morning glories for height and sweet alyssum to soften edges, turns a former home basketball court into a flower garden. In Winterport, Liz Osley drilled holes in the sides as well as the bottom of the watertight barrels so that soil doesn't stay soggy after heavy rains.

Even the littlest topiary lends substance to patios and terraces.
Kennebunk garden designer and topiary authority Anthony Elliott
prefers a relaxed look for his standard *Fuchsia microphylla*, opting to
leave some branches unclipped. Creeping Kenilworth ivy (*Cymbalaria
muralis*) tumbles from a companion pot in front of blue lobelia.

Left: On the southern coast of Maine, Penelope Marshall's potted phormium acts like a flag, directing the viewer to the bucolic pond just beyond. Helene Lewand helped with the design, planned to ensure a graceful transition from the wild to the tamed. In the background, purple loosestrife, now an acknowledged invader, entered the pond in the 1970s from a neighbor's garden.

Above: No soil required. An oversize compote heaped with pumpkins marks the entrance to Anthony Elliott's Snug Harbor Farm, in Kennebunk. What looks like weathered concrete is in fact a contemporary synthetic composite.

Left: Discovered beneath a bench in an old greenhouse, a circa 1900 American terra-cotta pot flaunts the felted "moss" that comes with age. To encourage a similar patina on a new pot, experts advise keeping the pot filled with soil and placing it outside in damp shade for several months.

Judiciously placed containers draw attention to a particular view or give structure to a small outdoor room. Potted topiaries (created from a wide range of plants, including ivy, boxwood, myrtle, germander, rosemary, and santolina) lend their precise forms and strong lines to the scene, as do cordylines, phormiums, and dracaenas, with their rigid, swordlike foliage. Perennials that don't demand direct sun, including hostas, ferns, and epimediums, can transform a neglected space (beneath a deck, for instance) into an intimate and appealing retreat.

Perhaps the chief virtue of container gardens, though, is their ecological benevolence. Pots make it possible to raise and enjoy plants without disturbing the natural landscape. Gardeners can revel in dahlias and daisies and still go lightly on the land. Indigenous species flourish undisturbed, and lakes and ponds remain free of undesirable by-products that conventional gardening sometimes brings. For example, silt, which can smother aquatic plants, and phosphorus (present in many fertilizers), which feeds algae, are non-issues. "If you avoid grading the land, you'll help

Succulents reveal an astonishing range of forms and colors, from glaucous blues and grays to variegated greens and reds. At Helene Lewand's Blackrock Farm, in Cape Porpoise, a succulent patchwork features everything from chartreuse *Echeveria* (top row, right) to rosy hybrid *Graptoveria* (bottom row, center). All prefer neglect to pampering, and all thrive in containers filled with gritty soil kept on the dry side. Non-hardy succulents such as these must be overwintered indoors.

The Decorated Dock

When it comes to gardens, waterside camp owners soon discover that they don't need a single square inch of land to enjoy their favorite plants. Docks provide space to indulge a passion for petunias or a hunger for herbs.

Along lakefronts, especially, container-raised plants boast virtues beyond eye appeal. Because no earth has been disturbed or amended, these micro gardens don't leach silt and fertilizers into lakes and ponds. Also, pots positioned on a dock are usually deer-proof, since most cloven-hoofed foragers would rather not walk the plank.

Where dock meets land, hardy ornamental grasses, including purple fountain grass (*Pennisetum setaceum* 'Rubrum'), compound the charm, waving gently in the breeze and serving as landmarks for fisher folk and sailors returning to the cabin at day's end.

Right: Ceramic bowls in paint-box hues line a porch ledge in Belfast. Because the bowls are not drilled for drainage, artist Paula Carter adds a few pebbles to each before filling with potting mix and pansies. She calls her gray house "a planned background for color."

Below: Container plantings bring the garden right to the water's edge. For a client on a midcoast island, Eileen O'Connor chose ornamental grasses and annuals that can be changed from year to year, among them verbena, dusty miller, *Dichondra argentea* 'Silver Falls', nemesia, and trailing licorice plant (*Helichrysum*).

Right: The color scheme may be monochromatic, but the scene is far from boring, owing to the contrasting shapes of 'Red Ruffles' coleus and purple fountain grass. Landscape designer Jacquelyn Nooney admits unapologetically, "I'm not into flowers."

In southern Maine, whiskey barrels sawn in half turned a formerly barren space beneath a deck into a cozy hideaway. Planted at the barrels' outermost edge, morning glories and scarlet runner beans receive just enough sunlight to work their way up the deck's support posts. Coleus and salvia along the building's foundation don't mind the shade.

the water stay clean," advises Mike Little, of the Belgrade Lakes Regional Conservation Alliance. "All the little hollows and contours absorb runoff. And if you leave the native grasses and blueberries, or plant additional ones, you'll have your own wildlife sanctuary." Well water, too, can be conserved. Although container-grown plants can be heavy drinkers, plenty of alternatives to thirsty roses and delphiniums are available. For example, silver-leaved plants such as lamb's ears, lavender, sage, and catmint require less moisture, owing to tiny foliage hairs that reflect sunlight and thus slow evaporation. And containers placed near freshwater decks and docks require no well water at all; gardeners can simply dip their buckets and cans into the lake and treat their plants to the nutrient-rich water.

Greeting the Season

Top left: Even snow is no impediment to window-box artistry. Candice Bray used holly berries and evergreen boughs to spread yuletide cheer. Cold temperatures keep the greens fresh.

Top right: Window boxes make it easy to garden every month of the year. A few six-packs of spring pansies from the local nursery can give way to summer annuals in vivid hues. In South China, Blanche Bourdeau chose pink pelargoniums, blue lobelia, and white bacopa.

Above: Autumn provides an ideal opportunity to showcase a different combination of hues; Anthony Elliott filled a terra-cotta planter with dried grasses, foliage, and hydrangeas in a Renaissance-style still life.

Although container gardening isn't difficult, plants will look their best if certain procedures are followed. Using the correct growing medium, for example, is crucial. The soil used in pots should not come directly from the backyard because ordinary garden soil is too heavy for roots to flourish instantly. It also may contain pathogens and insects. One popular potting mix recipe is equal parts loam, perlite, and compost. Every spring, the soil in large pots should be turned and aerated and amended with a fresh layer of growing medium. (Smaller pots are best emptied and filled anew.)

In Kittery, Jacquelyn Nooney, a garden designer and wholesale-nursery owner renowned for her daring combinations of grasses and foliage plants, offers these tricks of the trade. (1) Be sure the container is large

Window dressing takes a novel twist when you think outside the (window) box.

Top: A shelf with holes cut to the pots' dimensionsensures that the pots remain snugly in place when a nor'easter hits.

Left: A simple shelf affixed a foot or so beneath the base of the exterior window frame makes it easy to rearrange plants at a moment's notice.

enough to allow plants to reach their maximum potential—and have the maximum impact. "People don't think big enough," Nooney believes. "Large containers help plants gain stature." (2) Don't hold back on the number of plants. "Pack them in," she advises. A container isn't like a mixed border in which the gardener must allow for growth in years to come. Rather, it represents one of the few lawful forms of instant gratification—designs look smashing within a week or two. (3) Stay vigilant. Remember that plants in containers "are dependent on you for their life," the designer cautions. "Water regularly, especially during drought, and feed with liquid fertilizer once a week. You want to push the plants." (4) When it comes to choosing plants, don't worry about breaking any rules. Concludes Nooney, "Our season in Maine is so short, we should not deny ourselves anything."

Right: Cherry tomatoes, Bibb lettuce, herbs, and edible flowers join forces in a salad box assembled by horticulturist Warren Empey and conveniently sited within arm's reach of the kitchen.

Above: Grown in Maine as an annual, bicolored *Salvia greggii* 'Hot Lips' illustrates the revolution in plants hybridized for containers. Gail and Michael Zuck raised this showstopper at Everlasting Farm, the couple's Bangor nursery.

Right: Neatness counts. Galvanized cans in cubbies beneath a stairwell keep potting soil and amendments dry and within easy reach at a garden near Bangor.

V

Intermission

Garden-fresh fare

A break in the action calls for something special. How about a juicy tomato? Or a handful of strawberries so sweet they never make it from the garden to the kitchen door? Tender salad greens loaded with complex flavor, asparagus superior to that in the priciest restaurant, and grapes warmed by the sun: These and other delights taste so much better when you grow them at home.

Time out for a snack summer memories are made of: just-plucked tomatoes. America's romance with the homegrown "love apple" dates only to the mid-nineteenth century. Before that, these nightshade relatives were considered no better than poison. "The whole plant is of ranke and stinking savour," herbalist John Gerard wrote in 1597. Today, nutritionists say that tomatoes are loaded with lycopene, a cancer-fighting antioxidant.

This isn't news to Maine's gardeners, who have a long tradition of growing their own. What *is* news is that the national trend toward buying food produced thousands of miles away is reversing. Raising fruits and vegetables at home is no longer reserved for those brought up in the tradition of doing so. Everyone, it seems, is getting in on the act. Fifth-generation Mainers have been joined by newcomers "from away" and even by those who visit the state for just a few weeks each summer.

The reasons for this radical change in eating habits go well beyond good taste. For one thing, selection is much greater when you plant your own crops (try finding 'Black Oxford' heirloom apples at a supermarket). For another, many Americans now recognize that produce grown organically and harvested outside the back door is exceptionally good: The fresher the food, the greater the nutrient value (vitamin content decreases within hours of harvest). Increasingly, too,

Right: Vegetables and herbs share the bed with annuals for cutting, creating a feast for the senses. On a coastal island, Jan Moss mixes these and other edibles and ornamentals with painterly finesse.

Below: Edible flowers, deep crimson 'Oracle' mesclun, and cut-and-come-again salad greens offer an extended season of memorable meals.

Above: Bright red rhubarb, tender asparagus spears, and pretty chives herald spring. All three perennials form part of the backbone of the early-season vegetable garden. With its shallow root system, asparagus must be weeded carefully and faithfully (look for highly productive 'Jersey Knight'). Rhubarb, including the vigorous McDonald strain, attracts beneficial insects when allowed to flower, and it persists for years with minimal care beyond spring applications of compost.

people are realizing that it makes no sense to truck produce thousands of miles, burning fossil fuel, when tasty, wholesome foodstuffs can be grown much closer to where they are consumed.

Something else is new, too: the conscious desire of even first-time gardeners to work the land responsibly. "There's been a complete shift," notes Jean English, editor since 1988 of the *Maine Organic Farmer & Gardener*, published quarterly by the Maine Organic Farmers and Gardeners Association (MOFGA). "People have examined the data and awakened to the dangers of pesticides." The first line of defense against leafhoppers and flea beetles is no longer found in a bottle stored in the potting shed. It's in the soil itself. "Healthy plants are more resistant to pests and disease," English explains, "and building healthy soil is fundamental to healthy plants." Achieving a growing medium loaded with the microbes essential to productive soil is easier than it used to be. Premium compost, called "black magic" by gardeners who understand its importance, plays a crucial role. Ever-greater numbers of gardeners have learned that keeping a compost pile is no big deal, and even those who can't or won't make their own now have options. "Twenty-five years ago, no one was selling good compost," English notes. "Now it's possible to find quality compost in many hardware stores."

Left: Red-stemmed rhubarb chard mingles with shorter coleus and herbs in a vibrant pattern conceived by landscape designer Jacquelyn Nooney.

Below: At the Stonewall Kitchen Café, in York, Nooney paired ornamental plants, including grasses, tall papyrus, and crimson mums, with edible brassicas and herbs to illustrate the close connection between eye and palate.

Above: 'Liberty', 'Duchess of Oldenburg', and 'Winthrop Greening' apple espaliers frame Eliza Soeth and G. Scott Nelson's vegetable garden in Friendship. Eight strawberry varieties (including cold-hardy 'Cabot') dress up the trees' ankles and provide a staggered harvest in June and July. The tidy fifty-by-one-hundred-foot enclosure holds fourteen large raised beds (each fourteen feet by three feet) and thirty-six small ones (four feet square), with everything from artichokes ('Imperial Star', raised as an annual) to runner beans. Eliza favors raised beds because the soil warms faster, and they're easier on the back.

Above: Italian 'Chiogga' beets are as eye-catching as a candy cane—and, as their appearance suggests, they are reliably sweet. Also more sweet than sour is the soil that beets prefer. Soil with a pH lower than 6.2 may require applications of lime.

Right: High-intensity colors make a bold statement in Debra and John Piot's Sedgwick garden, designed in collaboration with Claire Ackroyd and maintained with help from Mary Cevasco. Leeks and beans share raised beds with 'Crimson King' nicotiana, 'Troubadour' yellow marigolds, and blue *Salvia farinacea.* Basil (including Thai and purple types), parsley, chives, various thymes, and other herbs give each bed a richly textured outline.

To raise robust crops, today's home gardeners have one foot in the present and the other in the past. They use row covers woven of tissue-thin polypropylene to protect plants from harmful insects, and greenhouses and hoop houses crafted of high-tech materials to extend the growing season. But they also recognize the value of traditional practices such as crop rotation, understanding how the preceding crop affects the succeeding one. They know that the main families of edible annuals—solanums (tomatoes, potatoes, and peppers), cucurbits (cucumbers and squash), and brassicas (broccoli, cauliflower, and kale)—affect the soil in different ways, using specific nutrients and playing host to specific pests. They realize, too, that leguminous plants (beans and peas) help restore nitrogen to the soil, as may crop rotation with certain cover crops or leaving the land fallow for a season or two. Most of all, they understand that to grow the tastiest tomato in town, it's important to ask a lot of questions, and ask the right people. These dedicated gardeners attend the many workshops and seminars offered by MOFGA and by the University of Maine's Cooperative Extension Service, as well as by the state's botanical gardens and parks. "Organic gardening is actually about thinking," Jean English concludes. "You have to be really smart."

The desire to eat better, and smarter, has left some gardeners in a quandary. They're loathe to give up the mixed perennial borders and cutting gardens

In South Berwick, a formal garden elegantly planted with a broad range of edibles and ornamentals perfectly suits the 1770 center-hall Colonial it serves. Marc Alterio divided the thirty-by-sixty-foot plot along a central axis, then balanced the look still further by choosing identical species for each half. At the end of a grassy allée, Romano Italian flat beans cloak a *tuteur* that lines up perfectly with an oversize pineapple, Colonial symbol of hospitality.

Berry Treats

Diets supplemented with berries can reduce, or even reverse, some effects of aging, research has shown. And by filling your berry basket with fruit picked outside the back door and consuming it the same day, you get a double bonus: maximum vitamin content and superior flavor.

Growing your own berries isn't difficult, provided conditions are right. Strawberries appreciate careful weeding to discourage pests that may be hiding in the foliage.

Deter them further by mowing or mulching all nearby vegetation. Cranberries flourish in full sun, in growing medium that's wet, highly organic, and acidic. You don't need a bog, but they won't grow in ordinary garden soil, either. Make a bed using two parts peat to one part sand, and keep the site moist. Cranberries are usually ready for harvesting the fourth year after planting. Just before the first hard frost, pick the berries and store

them in a cool, well-ventilated garage or barn, where they will continue ripening. Blueberries thrive in a range of full-sun settings (provided that the soil pH registers no higher than 4.8), including lakefronts, where they provide a useful buffer against runoff. For an extended harvest (late July through early September), plant early, middle, and late varieties. Among the best: 'Earliblue', 'Blue Ray' (midseason), and "Elliot" (late).

Cranberry-Raspberry Tartlet, at Chase's Daily, Belfast

Our Style Strawberry Shortcake, at the Riverside Café, Ellsworth

Artist Willy Reddick's prizewinning Blueberry Ginger Pie, made almost entirely with Maine ingredients, wows with its eye-catching crust.

they've tended for years, and they don't have time to care for an additional plot. One solution: a garden that marries the aesthetic with the practical, feeding the soul as it nourishes the body. Delightful to behold, resplendent as they are with flowers for cutting and groomed paths for easy walking, these multipurpose plots may have been inspired by the traditional French *potager* or the still fancier *ferme ornée*, although they can be compared only superficially. This is Maine, after all, and Yankee ingenuity holds sway. For example, a European-style family garden complete with *pétanque* court may include a brazier to keep mosquitoes and blackflies at bay (well, at least some of them), or the preservative-free lumber used to construct raised beds is likely to be recycled from other projects.

In ornamental kitchen gardens throughout Maine, vegetables, fruits, and herbs are selected with beauty

Heirloom garden pea 'Tall Telephone' boasts pods six inches in length, containing up to nine peas each. Vines can climb six feet (trellising required).

No need to bother with a vegetable garden if all you want is a few tomatoes. For a client down east, professional gardeners Rebecca Wheeler and Dean Worden planted 'Sungold' cherry tomatoes in sixteen-inch terra-cotta pots, each fitted with three bamboo stakes. Most suckers are removed, allowing just a few side shoots to produce heavily. An arborvitae hedge serves as a windbreak, and potted nasturtiums tied to *tuteurs* add pizzazz.

in mind but also with a keen eye toward tolerance for challenging conditions. Seed houses around the state, among them Johnny's Selected Seeds, Fedco Seeds, Pine Tree Garden Seeds, and Wood Prairie Farm, are helping gardeners meet the challenge. Cold-tolerant tomatoes resistant to early blight and spotted wilt virus share the bed with 'Kennebec' potatoes, whose large leaves help shade out weeds. Another potato, the pest-resistant hybrid 'King Harry' (a round, early-season white), is making life difficult for flea beetles, leafhoppers, and Colorado potato beetles. The disease-resistant strawberries 'Cabot' and 'Tristar' have earned accolades, and edible-podded 'Super Sugar Snap' peas and 'Miragreen' shell peas are touted for their resistance to powdery mildew.

Joining these state-of-the-art varieties are others so pretty that gardeners use them almost like paints. For red, there's 'Outredgeous' romaine lettuce with

a crimson ruffled edge, and two-toned 'Red Choi' pak choi, green on one side and burgundy on the other. For blue tints, artist-gardeners may choose from 'Blue Solaise' leeks, sky-blue borage, anise hyssop, or 'Winterbor' kale, as well as many cabbages. Chartreuse comes in the form of 'Galisse' oakleaf lettuce, common dill, and 'Lime' basil. Striking effects are achieved when these and other colorful crops are planted block style, in symmetrical squares, rectangles, chevrons, or diamonds. Contrasting shapes and textures enhance the scene still further, with vertical leeks complementing ball-shaped cabbages, and frilly 'Tango' oakleaf lettuce setting off smooth 'Deer Tongue' Bibb lettuce. "It's an amazing art form," says landscape and garden designer Claire Ackroyd. Talented gardeners have learned to "create pictures using paints and brushes that are living, growing plants. Herding cats is easier!"

Top left: In a demonstration of garden team-work, a sturdy shrub rose offers beautiful support to raspberries, one of the most carefree and productive fruits to grow in Maine.

Above: Apples displayed by Fedco Trees at MOFGA's Common Ground Country Fair (held annually in Unity the third weekend after Labor Day) represent a few of the hundreds of varieties once grown in Maine. Some apples are favored for snacking, while others are raised for cider, sauce, or pie. Choosing among just the thirty or so Maine heirloom varieties still available can seem daunting to first-time orchardists, but Fedco's experts are on hand to answer fairgoers' questions.

The results of so much planning and creative energy are stunning but seldom stuffy; precision counts but doesn't dominate. An unpretentious spirit prevails, and the setting—be it backed by towering white pines or sweeping ocean views—plays a leading role. "As long as you keep heights in the right place, I don't think it matters so much what is planted," the Orono-based Ackroyd believes. "It's *how* you plant that makes the garden. If you start with a carefree approach to arrangement and you have big, healthy plants and good soil, you will get a lovely, casual display." An expert in fitting gardens to their site (as opposed to the other way around), Ackroyd cautions that "Making a garden is an ongoing endeavor. You need a plan, but you have to be willing to ignore it. Sometimes, you have to try something new."

Left: *Pétanque*, anyone? After spending seven years absorbing the French lifestyle, Kristie Scott couldn't help but furnish her potager with Gallic flair. Planted in blocks, 'Purple Passion' tomatoes and blue-green kale and cabbages turn this Lincolnville garden into a painting, one that Kristie retouches every year. A brazier deters mosquitoes.

Top right: Midway through Pétanque tournaments, French pastis (for adults) and *citron pressé* (for Kristie's grandchildren) keep the game going until twilight.

Bottom right: Molded-glass bell jars, or cloches, protect seedlings in Linda Faatz's Gorham garden. The handy devices haven't changed much since their introduction at the Paris Exhibition of 1867, when they replaced much heavier leaded-glass plant covers.

VI

Amazing Feats

Rock stars, aerialists, and the world made small

It takes more than pretty flowers to make magic in a garden. What's needed is something extra—a touch of the unexpected, a glimmer of the truly awe-inspiring, or a glimpse of the fantastic. Maine's gardens don't disappoint: Optical illusions, aerial acrobatics, and nonstop arias by the world's smallest divas are just a few of the acts that draw appreciative audiences.

A cairn created by Ken Cleaves at his Lincolnville quarry garden signals a spot for quiet reflection. Since ancient times, stone pyramids such as this have marked graves, offered protection from evil spirits, and helped travelers find their way. Legend has it that when Hermes, Greek god of the road (his name means "pile of marker stones"), bested the goddess Hera in a debate, the judges showed their approval by piling stones at his feet.

Right: A fifteen-year-old mortared retaining wall supplied an outline for Shannon Amos's terrace garden in Kennebunkport. Garden designer Anthony Elliott chose fragrant creeping thyme, *Dianthus allwoodii*, and heath and heather to carpet the well-defined space.

Rough-hewn fieldstones sunk halfway into the ground frame Dale Tripp's seventeen-by-eight-foot kitchen garden. With a base of free-draining crushed stone topped by yards of fresh loam, the raised bed compensates for the property's wet clay soil. 'Bull's Blood' beets, rosemary (brought indoors in autumn), parsley, and 'Red Sails' lettuce couldn't be happier.

Rock Stars

For high drama, try this: a gravity-defying wall with clunky-looking stones that somehow stay in place for hundreds of years—despite earthquakes and frost heaves and often without even a trowelful of mortar. How on earth do they do that?

Among the many magicians whose dexterity has transformed the state's landscape, Maine's stonemasons are perhaps the most famous. It's a skill that wasn't learned overnight. Four hundred years ago, with help from nothing but the crudest of tools, and perhaps an ox, men (and not a few women and children) began to

Landscapers Dawn Marie Foster and Brad Ray defied conventional wisdom when they successfully enclosed a York County clients' garden (designed by Thomas Lovejoy) with a dry-stacked wall of chubby round stones, as opposed to more stable angular ones. Drainage pipes beneath the thirty-inch-thick wall keep the base from shifting radically during winter's freeze-thaw cycles. The structure tapers slightly inward, with the largest rocks on the outside.

clear fields for subsistence farming by moving millions of large rocks and smaller stones left behind by the retreating glacier at the end of the last ice age. Between 1750 and 1850, tens of thousands of stone walls sprang up throughout the state. Today, these sentinels of the past are preserved by gardeners and others who value them as works of art and as focal points and backdrops for mixed borders. Gardeners not blessed with an old wall have kept the mason's art alive by commissioning walls of fieldstone excavated from their own property or purchased from suppliers.

In the early nineteenth century, cut granite, too, became part of cultivated landscapes when landowners began hand-splitting boulders and using the blocks for house foundations, steps, and millstones to grind grain. What started as a backyard craft became a business, and by 1895 more than 150 granite quarries staffed by expert masons, stone carvers, and quarrymen from around the globe were operating throughout the state. Today, stone walls and furnishings born of remnants from granite's glory days (which ended in the early twentieth century as reinforced concrete came into wider use) are now integral to Maine gardens, both historic and contemporary.

Fascinated by the look, the feel, and the history of stone, sculptors and gifted masons have put Maine on

Opposite: A seventy-foot water feature created entirely from Maine stone includes a broad range of aquatic plants. For added realism, and to link the stream with the woodland beyond, landscape architect Bill Phinney chose boulders and rocks with matching tones.

Top left: A down east home-owner's love for fresh air and pizza led to a complete out-door kitchen and dining area sheathed in pink granite from the Francis Cormier quarry on Deer Isle. Landscape architect Bruce Riddell worked with mason Jeff Camelin to nestle the al fresco parlor into a niche created when ledge was blasted to make way for the owners' new house.

Bottom left: Large coping stones top a four-foot wall at Helene Lewand's Blackrock Farm on Cape Porpoise. Accomplished stonewaller Brian Fairfield created the fifty-foot-long masterpiece with rocks found on the property.

the world map of one-of-a-kind walls. "We're witnessing a renaissance in stonework," asserts William Royall, a Southport Island sculptor who, with a staff of two, produces the last hand-carved granite millstones in America. He says that today's creators of walls, walks, and garden hardscape "feed off each other and compete in a great marriage of art and commerce." Royall reasons that just as East Coast "rusticators" discovered Maine in the 1880s and fostered a boom in "cottage" architecture, well-heeled vacationers in the 1980s began purchasing old as well as new summer houses and demanding exceptional landscaping to go with them.

Royall's own story is emblematic of artists who decades ago began to meet a rising demand for garden hardscape. After carving his first stone at age seventeen (and spending not a little time on ski slopes), he discovered that whereas two-ton sculptures could be tricky to sell, his talents as a stonewaller were not. "People kept asking me to build stone walls," he recalls. The challenge was to render the practical as beautiful as possible. "Many walls represent craftwork," Royall observes, "but they can be raised to the level of art, depending on time and the customer's desires." Builders of walls are by necessity skilled scavengers, he believes. They hunt until they find just the right "treasure," as he calls it, then they put it all together. "Making order out of chaos—that's what a stone wall is."

In 1987, Royall switched from building walls to carving millstones (and, eventually, giant pumpkins and acorns). "Landscape architects began including millstones in their designs, and the antique ones were getting really hard to find," he recalls. "So I was fortunate to find a niche that provides my bread and butter and still allows me the free time to do what I

Opposite: This millstone won't roll and in time will gather plenty of moss. Sculptor William Royall **(right)** produces about fifty millstones every year at his Southport Island studio.

Above: Royall's granite pumpkins lend a touch of the fantastic to shady nooks and crannies where gourds could never grow.

wanted to do in the first place—sculpt original works of art." Maine Millstones produces about fifty authentic millstones a year. Most of them end up as focal points in gardens across the country, but a few are found in restored mills and schools. At the Skowhegan School of Painting and Sculpture, a Maine millstone grinds marble and lime—essential ingredients in the plaster, or slurry, from which frescoes are made.

About ninety minutes up the road from Royall, a Lincolnville quarry that fell silent in the 1930s once again teems with life, albeit of a different sort. Overloaded wagons and sweating horses have been replaced by cork trees (*Phellodendron amurense*), azaleas, and junipers from China. The sound of drills and shouts has given way to birdsong and spring peepers.

The man behind the magic is Ken Cleaves, who has spent three decades transforming the Heal Black Granite Quarry from pit to paradise. Incredibly, he has done it alone and without a single power tool. An old-fashioned come-along (a portable, hand-operated winch and chain), a nurseryman's dolly, a pry bar, wooden planks (for rolling stones downhill), and steel rollers (recycled from a conveyor found in a defunct factory) have allowed this independent New Englander to achieve his own vision of harmony.

Working solo with stones that in some cases weigh more than a ton, Cleaves learned to think first, lift second. "From the start, I knew I had to use my head, not my muscles," he recalls. His garden walls, composed of quarry leftovers, show painstaking planning. Stones selected for their unusual grain or markings, as well as for their shape, form patterns within each wall. "It takes a hundred stones before you find the right ten," Cleaves observes. Made of richly textured black granite (once favored for high-end gravestones), his undulating creations showcase the rubble left behind when the quarrymen called it quits. Iron wedges, lifting hooks, and other antiques unearthed at the site punctuate the walls and further tie this singular garden to the past.

Farther northeast, in Sullivan, two other abandoned digs—the Harvey Robertson Quarry and the Bragdon

Top: Ken Cleaves spent thirty years turning an abandoned quarry into a personal paradise.

Bottom: Iron wedges unearthed at the site punctuate his finished work.

Above: Spruced up with mosses and crevice plants, the quarry's heart now offers shelter to tadpoles and birds.

Below: Nearby, evergreens and perennials crown a dry-stacked wall that Cleaves built from quarry leftovers.

Quarry—also continue to yield "treasure." "Forty percent of the granite the quarrymen took out they threw away," notes sculptor, poet, and innkeeper David Buell, who, with his wife, Joanna, now owns the site. "Each piece has a natural beauty. Sometimes I leave the stone alone—it's perfect as it is. Other times I just smooth out a panel and place the stone among the property's old-growth pines. It's like walking into a cathedral."

Some special stones in the Buells' garden occasionally become birdbaths (a few of these he sells to visitors); others are transformed into sculpture. Knowing which stone to use for a particular project "is a magic thing—it just has to look right and feel right," Buell explains. "I guess it's the sense of permanence that attracts me the most. I'm not going to be around forever, but with these stones I can leave my mark. Granite really is the rock of ages."

At the pair of abandoned quarries he now owns in Sullivan, sculptor David Buell (right) lets the stone dictate the shape it will take. Some granite remnants from the quarries' early-twentieth-century heyday become birdbaths (above).

Take a Seat

Imagine a sofa that never stains, requires no springs or stuffing, and lasts for hundreds of years. When the "upholstery" is stone, you can leave your bench outdoors year-round and it will only look better as time goes by and mosses and lichens take hold. Stone seats can be customized to fit snugly into a wall, as Herb Staples did for a client in Belfast *(below left)*, or rescued from a quarry, such as the curvaceous slab that Bruce Riddell found upside down and covered with mud exactly where it had been discarded a century ago. Installed in a client's garden (furnished by Avy Claire with natives and shade-loving perennials), the "new" bench faces west for an optimum view of sunsets *(below right)*. Benches often come with their own backstory. A seat taken from the Newburyport, Massachusetts, garden of the owner's grandparents now sits securely in a Maine island garden wall *(bottom)*, a tribute to those who have gone before (masonry by Brothers in Arms).

Plants hold the power to soften stone and tie it to the surrounding landscape.

Opposite: Happy in the smallest pockets of soil, saxifrage looks as if it grows from stone.

Left: In southern Maine, evergreen English ivy (*Hedera helix* 'Baltica') cloaks a stone facade without help from wires or twine. Pruned when it approaches eaves and roof, the decades-old curtain of green does not harm sound mortar.

Below: Tough-as-nails cranberry cotoneaster (*Cotoneaster apiculatus*) scrambles up rocks in full or part sun, bearing bright red fruits in autumn.

Animal Acts

Although awe-inspiring, stone can be a little stiff. It lacks animation. For vitality, gardens need song and dance. Given the right habitat, Maine's wildlife is happy to supply it. Water gardens and ponds, for instance, attract frogs and toads, along with smooth-skinned salamanders and their rougher newt cousins. All feast obligingly on insect pests. Beloved spring peepers (*Pseudacris crucifer*, the state's smallest frog) devour pests, as well, while broadcasting the long-awaited night music that signals the end of another winter. Also captivating are pond skaters and water boatmen; microscopic foot hairs allow these and other water bugs to dance on the pond surface without sinking.

Above: A monarch caterpillar dines on swamp milkweed (*Asclepias incarnata*) at the Butterfly Garden.

Left: In Southwest Harbor, the Charlotte Rhoades Park and Butterfly Garden presents a kaleidoscope of ornamentals beloved by monarchs and other winged beauties. Volunteers, including Girl Scouts and master gardeners, who tend the garden favor aromatic plants and those with brightly colored blossoms, which are more easily seen by butterflies. Top choices include purple heliotrope, orange marigolds, magenta zinnias, and crimson cosmos.

Bee balm, butterfly bush (*Buddleia davidii*), baptisia, and other perennials hardy in USDA Zone 5 draw birds and pollinators to an all-organic cottage garden in Cushing designed by Helen Wisdom in collaboration with Gregory Moore and Kathleen Starrs. Pink hybrid rugosa 'Margaret Fleming' and a hedge of species rugosas that serves as a windbreak perfume the landscape, especially when breezes blow.

Bird and butterfly gardens, designed to attract everything from song sparrows to hummingbirds to swallowtails, boast an ebullience essential to every living landscape. Trills, arias, and recitatives fill the air from sunup to sundown, courtesy of cardinals, eastern meadowlarks, and yellow warblers, to name just a few of Maine's celebrated songbirds. Butterflies and other pollinators, including moths and native bees, pep up the scene still further as they flutter from blossom to blossom seeking nectar.

In addition to freshwater—all species seek it for bathing and drinking—birds and butterflies need food and shelter. Gardens with the greatest number of songbirds feature a wide variety of shrubs, trees, perennials, and annuals that provide nourishment as well as cover, at heights that mimic the natural landscape. Berry-laden plants, including blueberries, raspberries (both red and black), elderberries, and hawthorns, supply energy-rich carbohydrates, fats, and proteins. Some fruits are eaten almost as soon as they

appear; others (the berries from holly and *Viburnum trilobum*, or cranberrybush, for instance) remain on the branches well into winter, when they are easier to digest and taste less bitter. (Two things that bird- and butterfly-friendly gardens *don't* have are pesticides and free-ranging cats.)

Always, the diversity of plantings translates into the diversity of birds and pollinators. In Southwest Harbor, the three-acre Charlotte Rhoades Park and Butterfly Garden, open to the public and cared for entirely by volunteers, shows gardeners and birders the kind of mix that works. Beds laid out by landscape architect Bruce Riddell in the shape of abstract butterfly wings feature self-sowing *Verbena bonariensis*, as well as catmint (*Nepeta* spp.), coneflowers (*Echinacea* spp.), and Joe-pye weed (*Eupatorium fistulosum*). But of all the plant species that butterflies love most, "Butterfly weed and milkweed top the list," says Ann Judd, the garden's amateur lepidopterist and volunteer coordinator. "Butterfly bush is wonderful, too, but it's only

marginally hardy here in coastal Zone 4. We have to dig it up and overwinter it in a cold frame, or grow it as an annual." Parsley, dill, zinnias, hyssop, and various mallows are other good bets for butterflies, Judd notes, as are highly fragrant plants, among them heliotrope and pineapple sage. Heirloom species are especially valuable, because their perfume tends to be heavier than that of many newer hybrids.

For Ann Judd, most exciting of all is watching the faces of schoolchildren who visit the park to see meta-morphosis in action. "When we bring young students to the garden, they start to see things they've never noticed before. Right before their eyes, a butterfly hatches from a chrysalis, and they're totally hooked."

Opposite: Purple bee balm and blue anise hyssop (*Agastache foeniculum*), along with eight-foot rudbeckias and annual cosmos, form the backdrop of a birder's midcoast paradise. Woodpeckers, finches, warblers, song sparrows, and nuthatches flock here.

Above: In the midcoast garden of Ann and Hugh Aaron, pink phlox attracts hummingbirds, and yellow rudbeckias send a siren call to goldfinches, especially when the plants have gone to seed.

All Aboard!

Imagine a garden that's really the world made small, complete with a classic locomotive chugging through valleys and tunnels, across mountains and streambeds banked in evergreens and flowering perennials—all of it just one twenty-fourth as large as it would be in real life. In backyards across the state, garden-railway enthusiasts have achieved exactly this, to the delight of children and adults alike.

The hobby is a venerable one, having evolved from a popular interest in model trains that paralleled the development of the railroad industry from the mid-nineteenth century onward. In England, where garden railways had their start, model trains were often exact replicas of their full-size counterparts. The vogue reached its zenith on Britain's large estates, where detailed complexes, complete with bridges, station houses, passengers, and yards of track, formed intricate miniature landscapes.

Today's engines may be electric, battery powered, or even driven by steam, explains Doug Johnson, president of the Maine Garden Railway Society. "It's a hobby that's definitely family oriented," he adds. "Everyone gets involved. Often, one family member maintains the cars and the track—which remains outdoors year-round—while another focuses on the surrounding plants." Flowers and shrubs run the gamut from lilliputian *Iris reticulata* and creeping thyme to slow-growing dwarf Alberta spruce and miniature bird's-nest spruce (*Picea abies* 'Nidiformis'). Some plants are used as specimens, while others are grouped in natural-looking drifts or aligned to form miniature hedges. Children enjoy personalizing the scene with miniature passengers and track workers. Gradually, the family may add tiny dwellings and billboards.

Every year, the society's eighty members convene at one of Maine's twenty garden railways for an afternoon of train spotting and sharing trade secrets. Together, in a small way, they keep the era of the iron horse alive.

With eighteen hundred feet of track, Carl and Patricia Churchill's one-acre garden railway in Buxton is the largest of twenty in the state. In 1998, the couple removed a ho-hum flowerbed and replaced it with an astonishing fourteen cubic yards of rock, twenty boulders, and enough miniature evergreens, cranesbills, and tiny-leaved ground covers to create their own imaginary world. Structures, including covered bridges and station houses, take shape indoors in winter.

A Divine Dozen:
Plants Birds Love and Deer Don't

Above: Spider flower (*Cleome* spp.)

For many gardeners, the most amazing feat of all is keeping deer from devouring their plants. Although any tree, shrub, perennial, or annual may be eaten if the deer are hungry enough, some species are recognized as less vulnerable than others.

Shrubs

Apache-plume (*Fallugia paradoxa*)

Shadbush (*Amelanchier* spp.)

Japanese spirea (*Spiraea japonica*)

Annuals, Biennials, and Perennials

Bee balm (*Monarda* cultivars)

Bleeding heart (*Dicentra spectabilis* and *D. eximia*)

Catmint (*Nepeta* x *faassenii* and cultivars)

Cleome

Columbine (*Aquilegia* spp.)

Coneflowers (*Echinacea* spp.)

Foxglove (*Digitalis* spp.)

Globe amaranth (*Gomphrena globosa*)

Snapdragons (*Antirrhinum* spp.)

Left: Bee balm (*Monarda* spp.)

Above: Globe amaranth (*Gomphrena globosa*)

VII

Juggling Act

The secret lives of well-balanced gardeners

An artist-musician with deadlines to meet and songs to compose, an innkeeper committed to making dozens of guests happy every day, a veterinarian responsible for scores of four-legged patients: These are just a few of Maine's dedicated professionals who somehow find time to care for significant collections of plants. How, exactly, do they keep so many balls in the air at once?

Gardening can be the gateway to the future, Maine's students are discovering. At Belfast's Troy Howard Middle School, children enrolled in the school's Garden Project balance the season's squash harvest with a full course load.

The Young Scholars

Of all the juggling acts performed in gardens across Maine, top billing goes to the students and teachers who somehow find the time, the will, and, perhaps most impressive of all, the funds to incorporate gardening into their schools' curricula. At Troy Howard Middle School, in Belfast, children study economics, history, mathematics, science, and business management in a garden and greenhouse project initiated by Vicki Evans and brought to fruition by Don White. Students raise crops from seed, to the benefit of classmates, who enjoy the bounty in the school cafeteria. Student-raised produce is also sold at the local food co-op and at a student-run farm stand. In a student-published newsletter, they hone their writing skills and learn how to edit the work of others as they report on the progress of the current year's crops and marketing efforts.

"It's a totally integrated approach to learning," explains teacher Steve Tanguay, who with his colleague Jon Thurston administers the Garden Project. "At the beginning of the year, the kids attend 'boot camp,' where they learn the ropes and see all the opportunities. Then they're assigned one of eighty

Young agriculturalists harvest greens in February from Troy Howard's student-built hoop house. Along with earth science and composting, students learn economics and business management skills. They package seed from the previous year's harvest to sell at the student-run farm stand and at local stores.

different 'jobs'—everything from pest-control analyst to newsletter editor to accountant and farm-stand manager. All the roles are designed to meet students' individual desires and abilities." The program gets students away from their desks and into the community, on sales trips to the Belfast Co-Op and to the Maine Organic Farmers and Gardeners Association's Common Ground Country Fair. "These kids are heavy ribbon winners," Tanguay notes. The program itself has won plenty of prizes and has inspired other schools to adopt a similar approach to learning within an agricultural setting.

For the children, the message is clear: Gardening is anything but dull. "I've seen a ladybug eat an aphid under the microscope," wrote one student who went looking for action and found it on a leaf. Here, as the creators of the program say, is "Education so real you can see it grow."

The Muralist-Musician

In Augusta, Jane Burke's garden defies classification, just as she does. An artist, singer-songwriter, comedienne, and youth pastor (or "minister of creativity," as she calls herself), Burke maintains her office in a 1950s Vagabond trailer painted French blue, to "vibrate" with her electric-yellow mailbox, flower boxes, and daylilies. "I do like a strong palette," she explains, "especially pinks, reds, and yellows." Morning glories, striped crimson-and-white petunias, and pansies give her minuscule landscape an aura both straightforward and hopeful.

"I have a relationship with my flowers," Burke confides. "I find support in them, and they keep my outlook positive." The flowers—and their highly individualistic setting—reveal a lightheartedness recognizable in the many trompe l'oeil murals this master illusionist has painted for private clients and for Augusta's Senator Inn, where Burke's work appears throughout the complex. Musically, a similar joie de vivre is reflected in her CD, *Jane Loves Maine: Pop Tart*, and in her not-yet-complete pop opera, tentatively entitled *The Gospel According to Jane*. By keeping her garden to a manageable size, and by working inside its focal point, she finds all the time she needs to follow her muse. And by making use of containers packed with dazzling annuals, she creates a big impact in a limited space. (The containers also make life tough for the slugs that plague plants at ground level.)

Even though Burke's vintage trailer ("The Biggest News in Mobile Home History!" a 1955 Vagabond Coach advertisement exclaimed) isn't going anywhere soon, it gives this independent spirit the freedom to be queen of her own road.

A 1956 mobile home manufactured in New Madison, Michigan, by Vagabond Coach makes a one-of-a-kind focal point. Augusta artist and musician Jane Burke favors easy-care perennials and container-grown annuals in vibrant hues that complement the trailer and its adjacent, tented "siesta room." Garden furnishings include a 1950s enamel-topped table gaily decorated by Burke.

Photographer and writer Patrisha McLean takes time out in her midcoast rose garden, a feast for the senses featuring two hundred old-fashioned and hardy varieties; the robust crimson-purple Gallica 'Charles De Mills' (below) is one of them.

The Photographer-Writer

Also adept at mixing vocation and avocation is Patrisha McLean, known for her black-and-white portraits of children and for her newspaper profiles of midcoast residents from all walks of life. Many of McLean's commissioned photographs are composed in her nine-room rose garden, where more than two hundred varieties mingle with dianthus, lavender, foxgloves, and other old-fashioned perennials. It's a mix at once elegant and practical. Always, the most fragrant plants line the front of borders, where their intoxicating scent can best be enjoyed. Some roses, including Gallicas and other non-repeaters, double as trellises, lending all-natural support to sweet peas and clematis.

"The garden is both a set and an inspiration," explains McLean, hard at work on a book as well as a series of portraits entitled *Flower Girls*. "I'll look at a child's face and think of a flower that suits it." Lily-of-the-valley, for instance, might be just the ticket for a child with white-blond hair and pale skin. Soon enough, the question becomes, Does the flower personify the child, or is it the other way around? Although the issue will most likely never be resolved, it illustrates perfectly the integral role that plants play in McLean's life. "I love my flowers so much that I've combined them with whatever else I do."

Helping this busy wife and mother keep her all-organic "studio" looking ravishing is Faith Getchell, who, with rosarian Glenn Jenks, introduced McLean to roses in the mid-1990s. "I started with modern hybrid teas, and almost all of them died," McLean recalls. "Those that didn't die needed a lot of spraying, which isn't something I'm going to do." Finding the right plant for the right place and switching to tried-and-true heirloom roses and tough-as-nails Canadian Explorer hybrids have eliminated much effort and kept the garden chemical-free. Among McLean's favorites: the soft-apricot English rose 'Abraham Darby', the perfectly formed Gallica 'Charles de Mills', and the rare maroon-purple Bourbon 'Great Western'.

"Life is so hectic," McLean concludes. "My garden is the place where I can relax. It really is beautiful."

The Sculptor

Just as the garden can be a source of inspiration, it can also provide the ideal showcase for the fruits of that inspiration. In Rockland, sculptor Nina Scott-Hansen uses hot-rolled steel and a cutting torch to fashion whimsical birds and other beasts, some of which take up residence a few feet from where they were born. Scott-Hansen's well-weathered menagerie looks right at home alongside purple heliotrope, red bee balm, golden sunflowers, and other "action plants" that attract pollinators and fill the half-acre garden with life.

Although packed with plenty of well-groomed dahlias and thoughtfully selected irises, the twenty-two-year-old garden also plays host to more than a few volunteers, including nine-foot-tall woolly burdock (*Arctium tomentosum*) and native thistles. Scott-Hansen's live-and-let-live philosophy eliminates the stress, and a lot of the work, that go with more conventional, neat-as-a-pin beds and borders. Routine tasks are not this artist's forte. Because she finds mowing the lawn a bore, turfgrass is cut infrequently and confined to well-defined areas designed for walking and for the display of her sculpture.

Other chores, such as weeding, can wait until the mood strikes. "I'm not very good at following rules," Scott-Hansen acknowledges. "Gardening shouldn't be about work—it should be about having fun."

Enlivened with sculpture judiciously placed, a perennial garden becomes an outdoor gallery. Rockland artist Nina Scott-Hansen works at the site, using a cutting torch to create whimsical creatures, including gnomes.

The Hair Stylist

To manage a career and a garden simultaneously, it helps if you can eliminate the psychological boundary between vocation and avocation. "My garden is part of who I am and what I do," explains Kate Chapman, a Rockport work-at-home stylist known for tucking the occasional sprig of sweet Annie into her clients' freshly trimmed coifs. Rather than a thing apart, Chapman's garden is an important piece in the mosaic that is her life. "People come to me for a haircut and we end up talking plants," she notes. "Sometimes we'll go outside for a tour, and I'll give them a different kind of cutting—one from a favorite perennial.

Other times they'll bring me divisions from their own gardens."

When a client calls with a last-minute cancellation, Chapman heads outside her Great Lengths Salon and uses the "found" time to deadhead, weed, and tidy up beds and window boxes. Her son, Dylan ("my right arm," she calls him), helps with the heavy lifting. "Clients who've been coming here for a while like to see what's going on with the plants. They also like the wonderful, natural fragrance—it really is aromatherapy." Chapman sees a link between the way she works indoors and outdoors: "My specialty is curly hair, which reflects my philosophy in the garden: Let it grow, and see what it becomes."

Not your average tonsorial parlor: Tiger lilies, sweet Annie, and morning glories await clients at Kate Chapman's Rockport salon. Mia, the official greeter, enjoys the serenity of a summer afternoon.

The Animal Doctor

Although George Holmes can't say for sure that dogs and cats respond positively to his robust lilacs, dogwoods, and roses, he is quite certain that their people do. "I get lots of comments about how soothing the garden is, especially when an animal is very sick," the Northport veterinarian observes. One especially verdant enclave reserved for cats and their keepers provides a private place for saying good-bye. "They spend precious last moments in the cat garden," the doctor notes.

Back in the 1950s, the site of today's Little River Veterinary Hospital was "my father's hayfield," Dr. Holmes recalls. "Our sheep grazed here." Much later, after the clinic was built, the empty acreage held less appeal. "I couldn't stand that it was so barren," he remembers. So, in 1996, the clinic's foundation plantings took root, and work began in earnest: "The soil the builder left was all wrong. All of it had to be dug out by hand. I removed thirty-six wheelbarrow loads." Back then, "I only had Sundays off, so I'd head to the garden after work." In collaboration with professional gardener and friend Marie Keller, he softened the site's hard edges with flowering shrubs and climbers, including silver lace vine (*Polygonum aubertii*), which "grew eighteen feet in a single year."

These days, with more helping hands at the clinic and more time to call his own, Dr. Holmes finds that caring for the garden is easier and even more rewarding. "One of the best compliments I ever had came from a stranger who was attracted by the garden and drove past three times. Even though we have a large sign at the end of the driveway, he still thought the clinic was actually someone's home."

Top: Dr. George Holmes transformed the site of Northport's Little River Veterinary Hospital from sheep meadow to garden-bedecked clinic.

Bottom: Roses, lilacs, and fast-growing silver lace vine greet four-legged patients and their keepers. Skittish felines enjoy their own entrance.

The Innkeeper

Even the largest billboard wouldn't have a fraction of the advertising impact of his eye-catching garden, David Dickey believes. Passersby acknowledge that he may have a point. To reach Dickey's forty-two-room Camden Riverhouse Hotel, guests (and the curious) cross the Megunticook River on a footbridge awash in petunias, zinnias, asters, and other razzle-dazzle showstoppers. Cherry tomatoes tumble from hanging baskets, and pumpkins mark the spot where bridge meets parking lot. "I guess gardening is in my blood," Dickey theorizes

when asked why on earth he goes to so much trouble. After all, there are guests to look after and hotel staff to supervise. "It's just something I have to do." He chalks up the two thousand dollars spent annually on plants and compost to marketing. "The flowers make people happy—heck, they make *me* happy."

The garden's high-traffic location does pose certain challenges. Encouraging people to pick up after their pets is a big one. So is pilferage. "I have an emotional love for giant pumpkins," the innkeeper confesses, noting that children (and adolescents) do, too. A light

Right: Treats, anyone? Flagged by a 'Russian Mammoth' sunflower, an irresistible al fresco ice-cream parlor draws passersby to the footbridge that leads to Camden's Riverhouse Hotel.

Opposite: Innkeeper David Dickey uses drip irrigation to cut down on time spent with the watering can.

coat of petroleum jelly when the gourds are still young cuts down on theft, because "Most kids aren't into catching greased pigs." Just as pumpkins are synonymous with Dickey's garden, so are sunflowers, which entered the scene by accident. "When I first got started, I purchased several yards of loam that were loaded with volunteers," he recalls. "The weeds got pulled out, but the sunflowers stayed. I've been growing them ever since." (He admits to a particular fondness for fifteen-foot 'Kong' and the equally statuesque 'Russian Mammoth'.)

Part of the delight in doing all the work himself is in watching the reactions of visitors. "I can see how much they enjoy the flowers—and also that they think I'm the hired help, not the owner of the place. Their conversations are very interesting." To cut down on labor, Dickey installed drip irrigation the length of the bridge. Water comes from his own well, which is used exclusively for the garden. He also saves time by purchasing so-called self-cleaning petunias—long ago he gave up on geraniums ("too much deadheading"). When choosing a hanging basket, he does so with gusto, believing that "Bigger is better, since the larger the pot, the more water it will hold and the longer the display will last."

He might add that when it comes to gardens, big gestures are better than small ones. Dickey's fearless display catches, and holds, a lot of attention.

The Survivor

"I guess I'm a little obsessive," admits Robin Whitten, with a glance toward the thousands of daffodils, grape hyacinths, and tulips—especially tulips—she and her husband, Rob, have planted in their one-eighth-acre Portland garden. Whitten, an editor and founder of *AudioFile* magazine, collects tulips the way other people collect antiques and vintage wines. "I love the colors and the effects you can get when you plant a lot of them."

In 2003, Whitten had just completed her autumn bulb-planting ritual when a routine physical examination concluded with a diagnosis of breast cancer. "Suddenly, I couldn't be sure I'd ever see my garden bloom again," she recalls. "To get through all the surgery, the chemo, and the radiation, I was advised to focus on the day my treatment would end and on all the things I would do. So that's what I did. I thought, 'My garden is going to bloom, and I'm going to be there to see it.'"

Whitten did see her garden bloom again. She is delighted to add, "I expect to see many more spring gardens." Like other survivors, she came through her ordeal with a strong desire to give something back, to her community and to those faced with a similar challenge. Soon enough, while visiting one of Portland's cherished public parks, she had an idea: Why not grow some pink tulips here? And so the Pink Tulip Project was born.

After approaching the Maine Cancer Foundation, Robin and Rob Whitten and their friend Aurelia Scott planted their first public tulip bed, in Portland's Trinity Park, on Forest Avenue. Since then, with the help of countless volunteers and financial contributions from individuals and organizations, tens of thousands of pink tulips have burst into bloom in public landscapes across the state, from Lewiston's St. Mary's Hospital to the Kennebunk Middle School, where "Laurie's Garden," in the shape of an enormous pink ribbon, honors a

In Portland, Robin Whitten grows thousands of bulbs every year in her compact Portland garden (opposite). 'Angelique' (above) and other pink tulips have sprouted across the state as part of the Pink Tulip Project, founded by Whitten to help fight breast cancer.

beloved teacher. In 2007 alone, thirty thousand pink tulips were sponsored and more than $40,000 was raised for the Maine Cancer Foundation's Women's Cancer Fund.

Now overseen by a steering committee that includes Robin Whitten, Aurelia Scott, and a cadre of pink-thinking volunteers, the Pink Tulip Project hopes to "Cure Breast Cancer One Pink Tulip at a Time" (as the project's slogan declares), while raising awareness of the disease and honoring friends and survivors. Whitten, who has been known to appear at flower shows and fund-raisers dressed as a pink tulip, is ambitious. "We don't see why every community in Maine shouldn't have at least one pink tulip bed," she reasons. *Tulipa* 'Angelique', famous for its flamboyant pink petticoat, initially served as the project's mascot, and the more regal 'Pink Impression' has also starred in sponsored beds. In towns where hungry deer prey on all-too-tasty tulips, pink daffodils offer stunning alternatives.

Back in Portland, when May arrives and Robin Whitten looks out her kitchen window, she sees the results of her latest planting frenzy. But now she notices more than sprightly jonquils, intensely fragrant hyacinths, and luscious double tulips. She sees the power of flowers to give hope.

VIII

Great Escapes

Irresistible garden retreats

When Maine's gardeners want to disappear, where do they go? Not to London, or Paris, but to their own backyards, where irresistible hideaways range from the clever to the romantic. These one-of-a-kind retreats provide the perfect spot for listening to birdsong or practicing the flute, for writing a one-act play or enjoying a sauna. Some function as art studios; others become redoubts for the weary. Perched on ocean cliffs or nestled deep in the woods, great escapes serve up delicious solitude.

In Sedgwick, a custom-built pergola fitted with a cotton hammock from Puerto Rico promises sweet dreams. Crimson clematis (*Clematis viticella* 'Purpurea Plena Elegans') threads its way through a thick canopy of porcelain vine (*Ampelopsis brevipedunculata*). In the foreground, *Daphne* x *burkwoodii* stays tidy throughout the summer. Invasive in states to the south, porcelain vine is potentially unruly and should be monitored carefully.

Above: A homemade "apple tree" lends support to a Northport garden shed. Terry and Dianne Hire drew their design on paper, then had plywood cut to fit the pattern. A coat of plaster topped by latex paint conceals all seams; clear marine epoxy protects the finished product.

Top: An 1890s belvedere offers a ringside seat for viewing the action in York Harbor.

Opposite: A lakeside sauna beckons the weary after a day of gardening or exploring the countryside by air. Bruce and Beth Laukka built their heavenly retreat on a former campground in Hope.

Do-it-yourselfers who hunger for a room to call their own often mastermind these tiny sanctuaries. They pull out their toolboxes and set to work for other reasons, as well. Some need to flex their creative muscles or get in touch with their inner contractor; others may be searching for the perfect garden focal point. Frugal hobbyists who inherit an old woodshed may see an opportunity to restore a family treasure without spending a fortune. Maple-sugaring houses, smokehouses, and even outhouses may be candidates for remodeling.

Opposite: Boston ivy (*Parthenocissus tricuspidata*) cloaks a Camden gazebo almost completely. Tom Hopps, who created the cedar structure with help from John Grief, chose the deciduous vine because it bears no blossoms and thus attracts no bees. "When she was little, my granddaughter did *not* like bees," Hopps explains. Good drainage, a single plant at each post, and about three years are what it takes to get the look.

Above: In central Maine, Vicki Stewart worked with muralist and trompe l'oeil artist Jane Burke to create a garden shed that looks like a chicken coop. Wrought-iron strap hinges unearthed at the site and antique shutters tie the playful retreat to the surrounding farm, which dates back to the eighteenth century.

Left: Twenty oars, some barn red stain, and countless screws make up the "best little oar house in Boothbay," as contractor Don Viens calls the gazebo he built with his son Peter. Viens specializes in whimsical retreats created from recycled and over-looked materials.

Maine's nurseries off the beaten path serve up serenity in addition to plants. **Right:** At Sunnyside Gardens, in Turner, rustic furniture encourages visitors to take time out beneath a vine-draped pergola. Several garden rooms await exploration. **Below:** In Rangeley, Sunrise View Farm offers perennials, a full-service florist, and a romantic garden complete with mountain views, where lucky couples can tie the knot.

With help from her mother, artist Antonia Munroe, Fiona Fischer works on her brushstrokes outside her midcoast playhouse. Fiona's father, contractor Jay Fischer, created "Fiona's Folly" with remnants from building projects.

The truth is, planning and creating a personalized hideout can be as much fun as hanging out in one. The possibilities are almost endless: Leftover lumber can be recycled into a streamside outpost for watching wildlife. Cedar branches felled by storms might find new life as a gazebo cloaked in vines. A run-down chicken coop can be reborn as a tidy potting shed, and an antique boathouse can be converted into a peerless waterfront living room.

Interiors of even the humblest sheds are easily customized to fulfill almost any desire: A sink and shelves are sure to please the artist in the family, and a kiln will delight a potter or sculptor. Because plumbing and electricity can often be run from the main house, these and other improvements are all possible.

Right: An old door found in a cellar shows the way into Robert and Marie Stallworth's garden house and art studio. Recycled from a building project, the twenty-pane window affords indirect light. In the adjacent cold frame (fitted with another salvaged window), peppers get a jump on the season.

Below: Kathy Thyng takes a break on the porch of the tiny retreat she and Jim Beaulieu built in their Rockland backyard. Inside, a sink and shelves piled high with vases and supplies aid and abet Kathy's passion for flower arranging.

Top: A saltbox shed complete with Dutch door overlooks a Colonial-style cutting garden in Bar Harbor. Stored safely out of the elements, a wheelbarrow and tools are always close at hand.

Left: By Grand Lake Stream, northwest of Calais, Cathy and Bill Shamel's summerhouse offers an ideal vantage point for viewing wildlife. Screens keep mosquitoes at a safe distance without destroying the illusion of being outdoors. A tin roof supplies music when raindrops fall.

When planning a great escape, it's wise to remember that what's outside can be as important, and as enjoyable, as what's inside. A front porch, for instance, can make a small dwelling look and feel bigger. Here, beneath a sheltering roof, gardeners and their friends can read and think during a summer rain, or tuck seedlings out of direct sun while they harden off. A structure's sides and porch posts may come in handy, too, as backdrops and supports for hollyhocks or climbing roses. Screens will make retreats of any size appealing even at sunset, when mosquitoes go a-hunting, and in spring when blackflies can make life miserable. It's wise to keep in mind that, before construction begins, a building permit may be required. There's the tax man to consider, as well: Improvements involving electricity and plumbing may draw his gimlet eye.

Built when she was small, Emily Holden's Rockport playhouse now doubles as a focal point in the garden of her parents, Mark Holden and Melissa Sweet. Mark, an experienced boatbuilder, gave the charming hideaway plenty of headroom; Melissa, an artist known for her books for children, chose paint colors that echo hues found in the garden and on the terrace, which overlooks the playhouse.

In Lincolnville, Ken Cleaves gave his storage shed a slender silhouette
and peaked roofline to mimic the shape of towering pines.

Below: An Asian-inspired teahouse designed and built by Phid Lawless at his former quarry near Frenchman Bay features fiberglass pillars that won't rot and a fire bowl suspended over the water. A three-foot-square cutout in the center of the deck allows Phid and his wife, Sharon, to gather round the fire when temperatures turn chilly.

Practical realities aside, a private retreat can be a dream come true. Families can get away from it all without hassles: no waiting in line at the airport, no overnight parking fees, no dog sitter to hire. At a moment's notice, it's possible to entertain friends or watch an eagle soar. Here, inside a one-of-a-kind great escape, simplicity reigns.

Left: In Bar Harbor, Betsy Mills chose heirloom grapes, variegated kiwi vine (*Actinidia kolomikta*), and sweet autumn clematis (*Clematis terniflora*) to crown the pergola in her historic garden, designed by landscape architect Beatrix Farrand between 1928 and 1932. A recent addition, the pergola replicates a 1906 Farrand original created for a garden elsewhere on Mount Desert Island. 'New Dawn' roses climb the structure's substantial columns, cast in old-style composition concrete.

IX

Vanishing Act

Plants from the past, preserved for the future

Now you see them; now you don't. Some plants astonish with their ability to vanish then suddenly reappear. Take self-sowing poppies, for example. After disappearing for years, these sun-loving annuals quite miraculously (or so it seems) start popping up again in unexpected places. Underground, their seed has been sleeping, waiting for a passing plough or bulldozer to awaken them.

Garland delphinium (*Delphinium* x *belladonna*) gets along splendidly with "Dr. Vosmus," a circa 1900 climbing rose named by Donna Boyles, who discovered the parent plant growing against the doctor's nineteenth-century barn in Pownal.

Heirloom-plant collector Donna Boyles relaxes beneath an arbor with swing and side panels made by Steve Boucher of Modern WoodTech of Lewiston. In the 1820s, a farm occupied the 108-acre property in Pownal.

Other plants, including lilacs, roses, and many lovely perennials, play their own version of possum. Hiding in an old garden, near a crumbling barn wall, or around a cellar hole, they are not gone at all. They are forgotten—but not, it seems, by everyone. A half hour north of Portland, in rural Pownal, Donna Boyles is one gardener who has done her best to pull these supremely hardy, long-lost plants out of hiding. The acre of formal gardens that she and her husband, Jim, have created over the course of thirty years beckons with fragrant mock orange, cabbage roses, and old-fashioned phlox. More significantly, it constitutes a living library of eighteenth- and nineteenth-century annuals, biennials, perennials, and shrubs.

In mixed beds and borders, delicate pink-and-white columbines grown from seed collected by Donna at a young child's burial site date back decades. Nearby, a climbing red rose raised from a cutting evokes a much-respected local doctor who, more than a century ago, planted the bush alongside his barn. All around the Boyleses' garden, daylilies can be traced back to sixteenth-century China, where the fleshy roots were used as food. In lean times, the flowers could be dipped in batter and fried, and the leftover foliage fed to livestock.

"I feel this is Pownal's garden," Boyles insists, noting that her plant "archive" contains many species donated by generous friends and neighbors. The major emphasis in her gardens is her collection of heritage plant stock, which includes more than seventy-five perennials, roses, and shrubs. Daylilies (*Hemerocallis*) constitute her largest collection, featuring sixty named and labeled historics. She credits the Pownal Scenic and Historical Society, which she helped found in 1970, with sparking her interest in Maine's horticultural heirlooms. Her career as a plant sleuth began when June Tucci, a historical society member and fellow gardener, "had the idea in 1992 to sell historic plants as a fund-raiser," Boyles recalls. That first fund-raiser grew to become the biennial Pownal Heritage Plant Sale, which takes place the third Saturday in May at Pownal's 1886 town hall. There,

Among the many historic plants raised and recommended by Donna Boyles are bicolored columbines (*Aquilegia vulgaris* 'Tower Pink'), easily propagated by seed and just like those grown in England's cottage gardens four hundred years ago.

Top: Known locally as "Fourth of July plant," owing to its bloom time and patriotic colors, Russian comfrey (*Symphytum* x *uplandicum*) makes a big statement, standing four feet tall and wide. Hummingbirds adore the sweet nectar of this fleshy-rooted perennial.

Above: Tolerant of dry shade, hardy cranesbill (*Geranium macrorrhizum*) attracts honeybees to its showy magenta flowers. Deer usually give it a pass.

Boyles and her fellow plant detectives (dubbed the Pownal Plant Posse) offer everything from a large selection of potted heritage perennials (including *Iris pallida*, known locally as "Pownal Blue") to seed for such Victorian favorites as kiss-me-over-the-garden-gate (*Polygonum orientale*).

The Boyleses' garden serves as chief holding bed for the plant sale, which offers heirlooms propagated by a variety of means ("donor" specimens are never removed from their original sites). In the year preceding the event, seed for annuals and biennials is gathered by hand, placed in paper bags, labeled, and allowed to dry for a month in Donna and Jim's chicken coop. Once dry, the precious seed is repackaged for sale in small paper envelopes. Seed for columbines, tobacco plant (*Nicotiana sylvestris*), hollyhocks, poppies (including peony-flowered "Edna's Poppy," named for the former town clerk who found it in her garden), and other heirlooms remains viable for up to two years. Tuberous perennials, among them Japanese iris that arrived in America in the 1850s, and lemon lilies (*Hemerocallis flava*, syn. *H. lilioasphodelus*), so named for their clear, bright flowers and delightful fragrance, are lifted and divided in May prior to the sale. Heirloom roses, too, are cultivated on-site. To propagate these, Boyles takes cuttings thirty inches long and raises them in beds amended with horse manure and locally made compost.

Be it through seed saving or taking divisions or cuttings, propagation by individual gardeners or community organizations is often the only way to maintain a ready supply of rare species essential in the accurate restoration of period gardens. But there are other reasons why gardeners such as Donna Boyles go to so much trouble. Beloved by bees and other pollinators, heirloom plants are often hardier and more fragrant than modern hybrids. Moreover, with their unfamiliar forms and distinct coloration, "They make a garden unique," says Boyles, the editor and coauthor of *On Pownal Time: One Hundred Years in a Rural Maine Town, 1908–2008*. "And when we connect with the past we connect with others. Gardening becomes so much

Left: Ancient beauties that continue to please include striped Rosa Mundi *(Rosa gallica* 'Versicolor'), carried to America in the luggage of settlers from England, where it was supposedly named for Fair Rosamond, mistress of King Henry II (1133–1189).

Below: Another European import, eglantine rose (*Rosa rubiginosa*) boasts tasty hips, fragrant foliage, and arching canes perfect for dressing up a fence or stone wall. Out of control in some regions, it is still welcome in Maine's gardens.

richer." She warns that with population growth and development pressure, the opportunities for discovering lost plants won't last forever. "We have to get out there and find them before it's too late."

Just as plants connect us to gardeners of the past, they link us to key events, and people, in our own lives. The peonies that bring to mind the friend who gave them as a wedding gift, the tree that commemorates the birth of a child, the hollyhocks

Hollyhocks in Barbara Furey's Camden garden return year after year with little prompting. For centuries, gardeners throughout New England have collected biennial hollyhock seed in late summer, ensuring the perpetuation of antique strains.

Some plants need no help from anyone, thank you very much. **Below:** A peony-flowered poppy (*Papaver somniferum*) finds everything it needs between the stones of an old wall. **Bottom:** Wisteria cloaks a house long after the dwelling's original occupants have said good-bye.

Above: Siberian squill persists for a century or longer, paying tribute to the farm wives and nineteenth-century innkeepers who planted the tiny bulbs.

grown from seed collected in the garden of a beloved aunt: All become powerful symbols of what matters most, and all can be hard to leave behind when the time comes to move.

In Hope, professional gardener Robin Horty feels so strongly about plants as an extension of her family that she has moved her garden—not once but twice. The thought of abandoning her favorite delphiniums, poppies, Virginia bluebells, and yellow flag iris was simply "too heartbreaking." These were the flowers, after all, that had played a key role in the childhood of her daughter, Brooke. "I do not believe a garden possesses true magic until it has been explored, hidden in, danced through, and seen through the eyes and soul of a child," says Horty. Children "see deeper into things. They look into the heart of a flower and see it, really see it."

Refusing to leave the magic behind, Horty has discovered ways to save seed, dig and divide perennials, and prepare nursery beds so that plants can rest comfortably while a new garden is designed. She now knows she can take her garden along without decimating the property she's just sold to someone else. For example, plants that root easily (euphorbias, asters, dianthus, and phlox, among them) can be

In July, tall hybrid delphiniums and white valerian, along with daylilies, irises, and yellow loosestrife, bring magic to Robin Horty's Home Place Farm (opposite). Many plants, including feverfew and lamb's ears (below), are descended from specimens grown by Horty (above) in former gardens.

transported in what amounts to a horticultural jewelry roll: foot-long cuttings taken in early spring are laid horizontally on damp newspaper, set in turn on a three-foot strip of heavy black plastic, then rolled into a neat bundle, which is secured with garden twine. Periodically, Horty remoistens the newspaper, and in a month she checks for growth. Rooted cuttings are potted up and placed in a greenhouse or cold frame until large enough to transfer to the new garden.

Today, at Home Place Farm, where Horty raises cut flowers professionally, a new generation is discovering garden magic. Together with young friends and cousins, Horty's granddaughter, Natalie, plays among descendants of the eleven-foot delphiniums that her mother, Brooke, knew and loved. "My garden really comes alive through these children, just as my previous gardens did during my daughter's childhood," Horty observes. "This is what I most look forward to: my granddaughter, Natalie, dancing in my garden as her mother before her once did."

No matter *what* we do, some well-loved plants refuse to hang around. They bloom for a season or two and then call it quits. Among those famous for the one-night stand are hybrid tulips. The deceptively dainty-looking species tulips in many cases can be counted on to form dependable colonies, but many of the taller hybrids bloom for a couple of years and then shut down, refusing to send up more than a paltry leaf or two. The problem has to do with provenance: Although technically perennial, tulips balk at Maine's cold, wet growing conditions, which are nothing like those found in the plants' native Turkey. And because propagating tulips from seed takes years, gardeners reason that they have no choice but to purchase bulbs anew.

In Camden, Dimitri Stancioff found a better way. "In the beginning, I was shopping for tulips every year," he recalls. "But then the day came when I decided, *Enough. This makes no sense.*" A biochemist and authority on the uses of seaweed extracts, Stancioff discovered that from one bulb he could produce many. He could make his initial purchase last for years and have plenty of bulbs left over to share with friends and donate to charitable causes. "You've got to dig up and separate the mother bulb from her daughters," Stancioff explains. "Then you need to replant the bulbs at a shallower depth." He adds that, as a rule of thumb, offsets should be planted no deeper than three times their height, so that developing foliage can reach sunlight and send nourishment back to the bulbs.

In spring, he digs up the spent bulbs and separates them from their "offspring," discarding offsets that are pea-size or smaller. He places the bulbs and bulblets on old window screens laid flat in the sun and lets them dry for about four days, then he brushes away the loose dirt, removes the papery skins, and stores the bulbs in newspaper in his cellar. In autumn he replants them in nursery beds with a little 5-10-5 fertilizer sprinkled on the soil to move things along.

One to three years later, when the bulbs have matured, in midsummer he digs them up again and cures them in his cellar, then replants them in his garden in autumn. Come spring, Stancioff's second- (and third- and fourth-) generation tulips are indistinguishable from his neighbors' newer, store-bought cousins.

When it comes to home propagation, Stancioff recommends the so-called cottage tulips (single lates)

Dimitri Stancioff indulges his passion for tulips by propagating offsets from the parent bulb. **Opposite:** A ruby and gold Darwin Hybrid is just one of his success stories. Another, a red-and-white flame tulip, is descended from one already in the yard when Stancioff and his wife, Charlotte, purchased their Camden house in the mid-1960s.

Below: On the southern coast of Maine, stones salvaged from fallen walls became a house facade, linking the structure to the past and to the surrounding landscape. Entered through a gate crowned with 'New Dawn' roses, a kitchen garden flourishes on the site of a farm dating to the seventeenth century.

Below: On the southern coast of Maine, stones salvaged from fallen walls became a house facade, linking the structure to the past and to the surrounding landscape. Entered through a gate crowned with 'New Dawn' roses, a kitchen garden flourishes on the site of a farm dating to the seventeenth century.

and Darwin Hybrids. Disease resistant and blessed with sturdy stems, Darwin Hybrids include some of Stancioff's favorite cultivars, among them the cherry red 'Apeldoorn' and its sports, which he interplants with rare white columbines and forget-me-nots that he grows from seed collected on country walks.

By searching out and saving heirloom seed and by propagating and sharing perennials and bulbs, gardeners learn to see plants less as commodities to be bought and discarded at whim and more as fascinating characters in a broader narrative. Perhaps Donna Boyles explains it best: With plants come connection— to gardeners who have gone before, and to those yet to come.

Right: An all-pink theme sets the stage for May fireworks inside Treworgy Gardens at Friends' Corner, in Gorham. Magenta 'Karen' azaleas (among Maine's hardiest broadleaf evergreens), light pink weeping crab apples (*Malus* 'Louisa'), and a bower smothered in the foliage of twin Japanese maples (*Acer palmatum* 'Bloodgood') supply layers of harmonious color; a central path of finely crushed stone divides the space neatly. Audway Treworgy began the garden in the 1960s; daughter Linda Faatz carries on in his footsteps.

X

The Curtain Falls

Final glory in the garden

In September, as houseguests become few and children head back to school, the "audience" in Maine's gardens dwindles. Even the gardener in charge may not be around all that often. Other responsibilities beckon and, quite frankly, she (or he) is exhausted after months of weeding, pruning, and watering. And so the Quiet Season begins.

In autumn, tawny birch, golden grasses,
and hardy lotus ('Chawan Basu') cast a warm glow
in and around a pond created in southern Maine
by Joe Medina and Gary Devost.

Although the curtain may be dropping, the show is far from over. At one end of the garden, *Helenium* 'Mardi Gras' is kicking up its heels in a red, yellow, and orange costume that looks as though it's been tie-dyed. At the other end, against a golden backdrop of common witch hazel, *Sedum spectabile* wears a perky headdress of bright pink florets. Nearby, *Boltonia asteroides* 'Snowbank' flashes its daisy-like blossoms, and will do so for several weeks to come. Still waiting to make an entrance are Maine's native New England asters and their cousins "from away," promising prolonged displays of vivid pinks, mauves, and purples.

Above: A stone floor and weathered door offer a mellow backdrop for autumn's bounty. Native (noninvasive) bittersweet gathered from woodland walks decorates a wall; pumpkins and baskets of garnet-hued mums reinforce the harvest theme.

A Greek-inspired temple provides a classic vantage point for
viewing the ever-changing display at the pond created by
Joe Medina and Gary Devost.

Come autumn, plants we think we know surprise us, not least with their ability to change color as the thermometer drops. Ornamental kale, evolving from bland to brilliant, is only the most obvious example. More subtle are stonecrops that go from gray-green to glaucous blue, and hostas that set the garden aglow with foliage no longer green but golden. Roses, too, offer a glorious farewell as their blossoms take on a translucence no mail-order catalog photograph can capture.

Partnering the garden's late-season flowering perennials are ornamental grasses. In addition to giving the garden year-round continuity, "They catch the wind, creating movement as well as sound," notes Owl's Head garden designer Beth Long. A broad range of heights and habits is available to tempt today's gardeners. Feather reed grass (*Calamagrostis acutiflora*

Above: Wild sarsaparilla (*Aralia nudicaulis*) produces nutritious late-season berries that birds (particularly thrushes) adore. Maine's Penobscot peoples pulverized the plant's thick roots and included them in cough remedies. Today's gardeners use the historically important ground cover on embankments to hold the soil, but not in beds or borders, where it can take over.

Right: A wreath assembled from milkweed pods by Andy Pratt symbolizes the passage of time and the circle of life.

Above: At Pineland Farms, a business, educational, and agricultural venue in New Gloucester, landscape contractor Peter Lewis banked a brick walk in graceful *Pennisetum setaceum* 'Rubrum' and large-headed marigolds.

Left: Like a gilded cage, a Chinese lantern (*Physalis alkekengi*) "gone by" conceals a tiny ruby. Alas, the European and Asian native must be planted with care, because it can be invasive.

Left: The dried pod of a species peony (*Paeonia veitchii*) "looks like a Faberge egg," observes Rick Sawyer, who grew this crimson-and-cobalt work of art. "The pods last longer than the flowers," the Swanville plantsman adds.

Opposite: Nestled among late-season *Clematis tangutica* pods and fallen maple leaves, a hardy climbing rose ('Freisinger Morgenrote') grown by Muriel Krakar shows no sign of ending its colorful run.

Above: In early autumn, the bronze cones of hop vine (*Humulus lupulus*) form a fragrant corsage for Mother Nature.

Right: Queen Anne's lace (*Daucus carota*) concludes its life cycle with a seed head as finely wrought as a bird's nest. Each umbel produces up to a thousand seeds. Introduced from Europe as a medicinal plant, this naturalized wildflower is listed as noxious in some states, but not in Maine.

'Karl Foerster', for example), switchgrass (*Panicum virgatum* 'Heavy Metal', evolving over time from blue to ochre), and sea oats (*Chasmanthium latifolium*) bounce back after Maine's unpredictable winters. But non-hardy grasses, including fountain grass (*Pennisetum* spp.), are also worth considering, Long insists. "They cost about the same as annuals, don't require dead-heading, and give a garden wonderful inflorescence—the light sparkles as it filters through the blades. You get a lot of bang for your buck."

Just as they do the rest of the year, trees and shrubs form the autumn garden's skeleton. Without them,

A midcoast cottage greets the season in style. Window boxes cradle asters (*Aster novi-belgii* 'Odin Viking'), ornamental kale, gourds, acorus, and grasses (*Pennisetum* and *Carex*). Sage (*Salvia officinalis* 'Icterina') will come in handy when the Thanksgiving turkey arrives.

plants of lesser stature simply don't look their best. Landscape designer Bill Long, Beth's husband and occasional business partner, encourages his clients to experiment with the many species that hit their stride just in time for the garden's grand finale. Japanese maples, along with Ural false spirea (*Sorbaria sorbifolia*), enkianthus, and smoke bush (*Cotinus* spp.), deserve a wider audience, Bill Long notes. Most especially, European larch (*Larix decidua*) lights up the landscape late into autumn. "After other trees have lost their leaves, larch is still beautiful—it's one of the last to go." The Longs recommend looking beyond flowers and foliage to bark (river birch, for example) and berries (including *Ilex verticillata*) in the quest to enhance the garden's concluding performance.

An eye for the subtle—the reward of extended interaction with plants familiar and foreign—can help any gardener get the most out of the garden in autumn. After summer's pyrotechnics, spotting the tiny ruby inside a Chinese lantern isn't always easy. It's

Left: A backdrop of alders and antique apple trees ties Jean Moss's Waldoboro garden to the larger landscape. Plants gone to seed attract wildlife and hold the snow in winter.

Below: Feather reed grass, 'Hidcoat' lavender, golden juniper, and other plants resistant to salt spray and drought underscore a late-season view in the Boothbay Harbor region.

understandable, too, to walk past the jewel-like pods of species peonies. These and other plants "gone by" conspire in a ravishing, if low-key, curtain call. Not infrequently, though, they never get a chance to make an appearance, because some gardeners unwittingly cut back their plants and "tidy up" before fall's festivities have even begun.

In Waldoboro, Jean Moss has learned to tend her plants with a light hand. "It's really kind of fun to see what happens when you let go," this teacher and former nurserywoman observes. In Moss's garden,

Above: A blue jay feasts on tiny crab apples *(Malus sargentii)* in late October. Like goldfinches, nuthatches, and chickadees, he will stay around for the winter, lending welcome color to the off-season garden.

Right: Hostas cast a late-season glow at Merryspring Nature Center, in Camden and Rockport. The easy-care perennials (planted and maintained entirely by volunteers) thrive in low light, with little supplemental watering.

Right: Japanese maples dazzle with finely cut foliage in colors from the intense to the darkly serene. The deep crimson leaves of an unknown cultivar contrast strikingly against velvety moss.

Below: In autumn, paperbark maple (*Acer griseum*) features spectacular foliage in addition to distinctive exfoliating orange-brown bark.

rose hips sway on slender branches, while the plump pods of white false indigo (*Baptisia lactea*) burst with promise for a future, even more bountiful display. Dried stems and delicate flower heads left intact attract finches, waxwings, and other overwintering birds who seek them out for food and shelter. Years ago, Moss stepped back and let certain sections of her garden go entirely. "Seeing the bones—especially the alders and apples that were here before I came along—has been fascinating."

Jean Moss and others have come to the conclusion that the true magic of Maine's gardens may well lie not in what we put into them but in what was there all along: The elegant stands of birch, the lichen-covered stone walls, the sweet song of the white-throated sparrow. "All these things, some as old as the earth, and some with only a few hours' span of life, are not really ours except by a kind of legal quibble," Elizabeth Coatsworth wrote at her famed Nobleboro farm in 1944. In the Quiet Season, perhaps more than at other times of the year, our hard-won gardens are recognized as the illusions they are. On a sparkling October day, we see that even the costliest tailor-made landscape amounts to little without that which we will never, even briefly, possess.

Opposite: Ablaze with autumn color, Maine's native hardwoods bid farewell to another year. Maple, birch, and ash join forces in a curtain call few perennial beds can match.

Standing Ovation

We would like to thank the many generous gardeners who shared their work, their knowledge, and their enthusiasm with us. It is a pleasure to be with those who are excited about what nature has to offer and who clearly enjoy each day to the fullest.

Our gratitude also goes to our editors at *Better Homes & Gardens* Garden Group, and to *Cottage Living*, *La Vie Claire*, and *Country Living Gardener*, where some of the gardens included in this book first appeared.

Our hats are off, as well, to the many professional gardeners and educators who so graciously answered Rebecca's endless questions and who granted Lynn repeated access to their gardens and plant collections, among them Rick Sawyer, Thomas Lovejoy, Jacquelyn Nooney, Robin Horty, Marie Keller, George Holmes, Helene Lewand, Anthony Elliott, Ken Liberty, Bob and Linda Bangs, Sue Keating, Beth and Bill Long, Steve Tanguay, Don White, Jon Thurston, and our dear friend Sharon Lovejoy. We are especially grateful to Jean English for sharing her knowledge of organic gardening.

This book would not have been possible without the support of our editor, Karin Womer, the talent of

Clockwise from top left: Jacquelyn Nooney, Linda Bangs, Marie Keller, Jean English and daughter Saima Sidik, and Rick Sawyer

our designer, Faith Hague, and the practiced eye of our copy editor, Barbara Feller-Roth. Our thanks to you all.

From Lynn, special thanks go to Muriel Krakar for fifteen years of friendship and gardening wisdom. And to Barry Way for his patience, love, and understanding when she's "on call" in all seasons and continually rushing to gardens across the state; to Florence and Sy Karlin, youthful parents and biggest fans, for their never-ending support, giving nature, garden-tour companionship, and pied-à-terre; Lawrence and Donna Way, for access to their century-old lilac as well as for the enthusiasm and insight that come with forty-five years in the nursery business; and Timmy the Maine coon cat, whose greeting is as warm after one week as it is after one hour. From Rebecca, thanks go to Bart Wood, for his insights into the world of birds and for his friendship; to Kate Barnes, for permission to quote her mother, Elizabeth Coatsworth; and to Terry and Dianne Hire, gardeners at once fearless, talented, and kind. Heartfelt thanks go to Sean Fay for his technical expertise, and especially for his smile. Most of all, thank you, Joe, for being there.

Clockwise from top left: Helene Lewand, Lawrence "Bub" Way, Terry and Dianne Hire, and Thomas Lovejoy

Behind the Scenes

This resource list gives contact information for individuals and businesses mentioned in the preceding pages. All telephone area codes are 207. Call ahead for hours and dates of operation.

Garden Designers, Landscape Architects, Consultants

Claire Ackroyd
(landscape and garden designer)
80 Stillwater Ave.
Orono, ME 04473
866-5825
www.claireackroyd.com

Bob Bangs
(landscape and garden designer)
1709 Broadway
Bangor, ME 04401
941-9898
www.windsweptgardens.com

Mary Cevasco
(garden designer and consultant)
517 Sunshine Rd.
Deer Isle, ME 04627
348-2523

Ken Cleaves (garden consultant)
98 Quarry Rd.
Lincolnville, ME 04849
763-4019

Anthony Elliott
(garden designer)
Snug Harbor Farm
87 Western Ave.
Kennebunk, ME 04043
967-2414

Sue Hatch
(garden designer)
P.O. Box 289
Islesboro, ME 04848
734-6407

Kathie Iannicelli
(garden designer)
P.O. Box 131
Monhegan Island, ME 04852

Helene Lewand
(garden designer)
Blackrock Farm
293 Goose Rocks Rd.
Kennebunkport, ME 04046
967-5783
www.blackrockfarm.net

Beth & Bill Long
(garden design and landscaping)
North Shore Drive
Owls Head, ME 04854
593-9059

Thomas Lovejoy
(landscape architect)
Telov1@aol.com

Gregory Moore & Kathleen Starrs
(garden design and landscaping)
Hands and Knees Gardens
67 McCarter Point Rd.
Cushing, ME 04563
354-6841

Jacquelyn Nooney
(landscape and garden designer)
Jacquelyn Nooney Landscape, Inc.
18 Stevenson Rd.
Kittery, ME 03904
439-6075
www.jnlinc.com

Bill Phinney
(landscape architect)
15 Lee St.
Wiscasset, ME 04578
882-6226

Anna Remsen
(garden designer)
Seasons Downeast Designs
62 Meadow Rd.
Rockport, ME 04856
236-4147
www.seasonsdowneast.com

Bruce John Riddell
(landscape architect)
27 Pine St.
Bar Harbor, ME 04609
288-9668
www.landartdesigner.com

Lee Schneller
(garden designer)
P.O. Box 333
South Thomaston, ME 04858
594-7311
www.leeschneller.com

Nurseries & Garden Shops

Blackrock Farm
293 Goose Rocks Rd.
Kennebunkport, ME 04046
967-5783
www.blackrockfarm.net

Endless Summer Flower Farm
57 East Fork Rd.
P.O. Box 1225
Camden, ME 04843
236-8752
www.endlesssummerflowerfarm.com

Everlasting Farm
2140 Essex St.
Bangor, ME 04401
947-8836
www.everlastingfarm.com

Fernwood Nursery & Gardens
433 Cross Rd.
Swanville, ME 04915
338-4100; 322-6420

Fieldstone Gardens, Inc.
55 Quaker Lane
Vassalboro, ME 04989
923-3836
www.fieldstonegardens.com

The Lavender Rose Garden
361 Waldoboro Rd. (Rte. 220)
Friendship, ME 04547

Maine Cottage Garden
6 Dodge Corner Rd.
Strong, ME 04983
684-3400
www.mainecottagegarden.com

Seasons Downeast Designs
62 Meadow Rd.
Rockport, ME 04856
236-4147
www.seasonsdowneast.com

Snug Harbor Farm
87 Western Ave.
Kennebunk, ME 04043
967-2414

Sunnyside Gardens
500 N. Parish Rd.
Turner, ME 04282
225-3998
www.sunnysidegardens.com

Sunrise View Farm
2936 Main St.
Rangeley, ME 04970
864-2117

Sweet Pea Gardens
1278 Surry Rd.
Surry, ME 04684
667-6751; 667-4730
www.sweetpeagardens.com

Windswept Gardens
1709 Broadway
Bangor, ME 04401
941-9898
www.windsweptgardens.com

Societies, Organizations, Helpful Web Sites

Belgrade Lakes Regional Conservation Alliance
172 Main St.
Belgrade Lakes, ME 04918
495-6039
www.belgradelakes.org

Cellardoor Vineyard
367 Youngtown Rd.
Lincolnville, ME 04849
www. mainewine.com
(Experts on hand to answer gardeners' questions)

Down East's Web site
www.downeast.com
Publisher's site periodically includes features relating to Maine gardens and gardeners

Societies, Organizations, Helpful Web Sites
continued

The Troy Howard Middle School Garden Project
173 Lincolnville Ave.
Belfast, ME 04915
338-3320, ext. 119;
   garden@SAD34.net
www.SAD34.net/garden
(Seed packets on sale at Mr. Paperback, Belfast Plaza; 338-2735)

Leslie Land
Gardening and cooking blog
www.leslieland.com

Maine Daylily Society
Susan Shaw, President
13 Mill St.
Camden, ME 04843
236-4085

Maine Garden Railway Society
Douglas R. Johnson, President
P.O. Box 355
Hollis Center, ME 04042
929-4015

Maine Organic Farmers & Gardeners Association
P.O. Box 170
Unity, ME 04988
568-4142
www.mofga.org

Netherlands Flower Bulb Information Center
www.bulb.com

Pink Tulip Project
www.mainecancer.org/pinktulips

Garden Products & Services

Brothers in Arms Masonry
James Nelson
342-4258; 323-2004

Campania International
   (planters and ornaments)
www.campaniainternational.com

Lunaform
   (hand-turned garden urns)
66 Cedar Lane
Sullivan, ME 04664
422-0923
www.lunaform.com

Maine Millstones
98 Pratts Island Rd.
P.O. Box 228
Southport, ME 04576
633-6091
www.mainemillstones.com

Modern WoodTech
   (garden furnishings)
1990 Lisbon Rd.
Lewiston, ME 04240
786-3304
www.modernwoodtech.com

Andy Pratt (wreaths)
1206 Old Stage Rd.
Woolwich, ME 04579
882-9641

Herb Staples
   (mason)
Swan Lake Ave.
P.O. Box 284
Belfast, ME 04915
338-9026

Sunrise View Farm
   (weddings)
2936 Main St.
Rangeley, ME 04970
864-2117

D. P. Viens
   (sheds & outbuildings)
P.O. Box 74
Boothbay, ME 04573
633-6451; 380-1963

Garden Tours

A comprehensive list of garden tours throughout Maine appears annually in the Early Summer issue of *People, Places & Plants* magazine (www.ppplants.com). The same issue contains up-to-date directories of garden centers, landscapers, and public gardens to visit.

For brief descriptions of the state's public gardens, visit the Maine Office of Tourism Web site (www.visitmaine.com/seasonaltrails/garden_landscape.php) and download their brochure on the Maine Garden and Landscape Trail.

Seed Suppliers

Fedco Seeds and Fedco Trees
P.O. Box 520
Waterville, ME 04903
873-7333
www.fedcoseeds.com

Johnny's Selected Seeds
955 Benton Ave.
Winslow, ME 04901
877-564-6697
www.johnnyseeds.com

Pinetree Garden Seeds
P.O. Box 300
New Gloucester, ME 04260
926-3400
www.superseeds.com

Wood Prairie Farm
49 Kinney Rd.
Bridgewater, ME 04735
800-829-9765
www.woodprairie.com

Artists

Paul & Ann Breeden
   (visual artists)
Willowbrook Garden and Spring
   Woods Gallery
19 Willowbrook Lane
Sullivan, ME 04664
422-3007
www.willowbrookgarden.com

Jane Burke
   (muralist)
50 Gage St.
Augusta, ME 04330
www.mainemurals.com

Eric Hopkins
   (visual artist)
www.erichopkins.com
Eric Hopkins Gallery, North Haven
   (summer only)
Hopkins Wharf, P.O. Box 526
North Haven, ME 04853
867-2229
Eric Hopkins Gallery, Rockland
   (year-round)
21 Winter St., Suite 3
Rockland, ME 04841
594-1996

Patrisha McLean
   (children's photographer)
www.patrishamclean.com

William L. Royall
   (sculptor)
98 Pratts Island Rd.
P.O. Box 228
Southport, ME 04578
633-6091
www.williamroyallsculpture.com

Nina Scott-Hansen
   (sculptor)
594-0630
Represented by Harbor Square
   Gallery
374 Main St.
Rockland ME 04841
594-8700
www.harborsquaregallery.com

Index

pak choi 'Red Choi', 87
pansy, 47, 57, 66, 68, 116
papyrus, 77
parsley, 54, 78, 92, 109
paths in gardens, 24–25, 46
pea: 'Miragreen' , 86; 'Super Sugar Snap', 86; 'Tall Telephone', 84
pelargonium, 68. *See also* geranim
peony (*Paeonia*), 22–23, 146, 164; bud blast in, 23; 'Sarah Bernhart', 23; species (*Paeonia veitchii*), 160, 164
People, Places, Plants magazine, 172
pergola, 127, 132, 139
peppers, 134, 159
pesticides, 76, 108
petunia, 65, 116, 122, 123
Phinney, Bill, 95, 170
phlox, 49, 109, 143, 148
phormium, 63, 64
pine, 41, 88, 138; Dragon's eye (*Pinus densiflora* 'Oculus-draconis'), 35; white, 43
Pineland Farms, 159
Pine Tree Garden Seeds, 86, 173
Pine Tree State Arboretum, 19
Pink Tulip Project, 124–25, 172
Piot, Debra and John, 78
pitcher plant, 34–35; native (*Sarracenia purpurea*), 35
planting times, 14
plumule, 15
polypropylene plant covering, 81
ponds, examples of, 9, 52, 139, 155, 156–57
poppy (*Papaver*), 19, 41, 144, 148; Himalayan blue (*Meconopsis grandis*), 55; *P. somniferum*, 50, 147
porcelain vine (*Ampelopsis brevipedunculata*), 127
potato: 'Kennebec' and 'King Harry', 86
potting mix recipe, 69
Pownal Heritage Plant Sale, 143
Pownal Scenic and Historical Society, 143
Pratt, Andy, 158, 172
primrose, 18, 59; candelabra (*Primula* X *bulleesiana*), 24; cape (*Streptocarpus*), 60
pumpkin, 122–23, 156; stone, 96

quarries, 95, 98–99
quarry gardens, 98–100, 139
Queen Anne's lace (*Daucus carota*), 50, 160
queen-of-the-prairie (*Filipendula rubra*), 49

radicle, 15
raised beds, 50, 77, 92; examples of, 33, 84
Rangeley Public Library, 58
raspberry, 87, 108
Ray, Brad, 93
Reddick, Willy, 83
Remsen, Anna, 170
rhododendron, 36, 41
rhubarb, 74, 77
Rich, Jean and Robert, 13
Richardson, Laura and Blaine, 58
Riddell, Bruce John, 95, 101, 108, 170
Riverside Café, 83
rodents, 13
rose (*Rosa*), 11, 21, 41, 42, 43, 55, 67, 87, 121, 136, 143, 144, 158, 160; 'Abraham Darby', 117; Canadian Explorer hybrids, 117; 'Charles De Mills', 117; cultivating,

28–29; 'Cressida', 29; David Austin's English, 29; "Dr. Vosmus," 141; eglantine (*R. rubiginosa*), 145; 'Freisinger Morgenrote', 160; Gallicas, 117; 'Golden Celebration', 28; 'Graham Thomas', 29; 'Great Western', 117; heirloom, 117; 'Hermosa', 29; *rugosa*, 107; 'Mme. Hardy', 29; 'Mary Rose', 29; 'New Dawn', 139, 152; Rosa Mundi (*R. Gallica* 'Versicolor'), 145; 'William Baffin', 28, 29
rose campion, 42
rosehips, 166
rosemary, 64, 92
Royall, William L., 96–98, 173
rudbeckia, 18, 19, 109
Ruskin, John, 19

sage (*Salvia*), 60, 67, 70, 109; pineapple, 109; *S. farinacea*, 78; *S. officinalis* 'Icterina', 162
St. Mary's Hospital, 124
salad greens, 73, 74, 87, 114
santolina, 64
sarsaparilla, wild (*Aralia nudicaulis*), 158
Sawyer, Rick, 159
saxifrage, 102
Schneller, Lee, 53, 170
Scott, Kristie, 89
Scott-Hansen, Nina, 118, 173
Seasons Downeast Designs, 171
Sedum spectabile, 156
seed suppliers in Maine, 86, 173
shadbush (*Amelanchier*), 111
Shamel, Cathy and Bill, 135
Shaw, Susan, 30, 31
silver lace vine (*Polygonum aubertii*), 121
Skowhegan School of Painting and Sculpture, 98
skunk cabbage, 24
smoke bush (*Cotinus*), 162
snapdragon (*Antirrhinum*), 58, 111
Snug Harbor Farm, 63, 171
Soeth, Eliza, 77
soil nutrients, 81
solanums, 81
Solomon's seal, 36
sparrow, song, 109
spider flower (*Cleome*), 111
spirea, Japanese (*Spiraea japonica*), 111
spring peeper (*Pseudacris crucifer*), 105
spruce, 50, 111; bird's-nest (*Picea abies* 'Nidiformis'), 110
squash, 74; butternut, 15
squill, Siberian, 147
Stallworth, Robert and Marie, 134
Staples, Herb, 101, 172
Stancioff, Dimitri, 150–52
Starrs, Kathleen, 107, 170
Stewart, Vicki, 131
stone: benches and seats, 22, 101; cairn, 90; coping, 95; in gardens, 91–103, 152–53; millstones, 96–98; in outdoor kitchen, 95; walls, 92–99, 101, 166
stonecrop, 158
Stonewall Kitchen, 53, 77
strawberry, 73, 82–83, 84, 162; 'Cabot', 77, 86; 'Tristar', 86
structure ("bones") in gardens, 42, 64, 166
succulents, 64
sunflower, 118, 122; 'Kong' and 'Russian

Mammoth', 123
Sunnyside Gardens, 132, 171
Sunrise View Farm, 132, 171, 172
Sweet, Melissa, 137
sweet Annie, 120
sweet pea, 117
Sweet Pea Gardens, 60, 171

Tanguay, Steve, 114, 115
thistle, 118
thrushes, 158
Thuja occidentalis, 49
Thuya Garden, 19
Thurston, Jon, 114
thyme, 78, 110; creeping, 92
Thyng, Kathy, 134
Tiarella 'Pink Pearls', 51
tobacco plant (*Nicotiana sylvestris*), 144
tomato, 73, 81, 84; cherry, 59, 70, 86, 122; 'Purple Passion', 89
topiary, 45, 49; in pots, 62, 64
trees, 161–62, 166. *See also* individual species
trellis, 49, 117; examples of, 84, 85, 176
Trewogy, Audway, 152
Trewogy Gardens, 152–53
trillium, 18, 41
Trinity Park (Portland), 124
Tripp, Dale, 92
Troy Howard Middle School Garden Project, 113–14, 172
tulip (*Tulipa*), 10, 124, 125, 149–152; 'Apeldoorn', 152; propagation of, 150–52; cottage, 150; Darwin Hybrids, 152
tuteur, 81, 86

University of Maine Cooperative Extension Service, 81
Urick, Christine and Dennis, 84
USDA climate zones, 14

valerian, 148
vegetable gardens, 73–89
verbena, 66; *V. bonariensis*, 108
Viburnum trilobum berries, 108
Viens, Don P. and Peter, 131, 172
Vogt, Frank and Janie, 50

warblers, 109
water feature, 94
waxwings, 166
Wheeler, Rebecca, 86
Whitten, Robin, 124
Wild Gardens of Acadia, 19
Willowbrook Garden and Spring Woods Gallery, 52
Windswept Gardens, 23, 29, 171
Wisdom, Helen, 107
wisteria, Japanese, 39, 147
witch hazel, 156
woodpeckers, 109
Wood Prairie Farm, 86, 173
Worden, Dean, 86

yarrow, 42
yew hedge, 43

zinnia, 105, 109, 122